D0581566

JKT L
(Hus)

WHAT IS
HISTORY TEACHING?

7day

HAROLD SCHOOLS LIBRARY
S. MARTIN'S COLLEGE
LANCASTER

033 519 6381

WHAT IS HISTORY TEACHING?

Language, ideas and meaning
in learning about the past

Chris Husbands

Open University Press
Buckingham · Philadelphia

Open University Press
Celtic Court
22 Ballmoor
Buckingham
MK18 1XW

and
1900 Frost Road, Suite 101
Bristol, PA 19007, USA

First Published 1996
Reprinted 1998

Copyright © Chris Husbands 1996

All rights reserved. Except for the quotation of short passages for the
purpose of criticism and review, no part of this publication may be
reproduced, stored in a retrieval system, or transmitted, in any form or by
any means, electronic, mechanical, photocopying, recording or otherwise,
without the prior written permission of the publisher or a licence from the
Copyright Licensing Agency Limited. Details of such licences (for
reprographic reproduction) may be obtained from the Copyright Licensing
Agency Ltd of 90 Tottenham Court Road, London, W1P 9HE.

A catalogue record of this book is available from the British Library

ISBN   0 335 19638 1 (pb)   0 335 19639 X (hb)

Library of Congress Cataloging-in-Publication Data
Husbands, Christopher R.
    What is history teaching? : language, ideas, and meaning in learning
about the past / Chris Husbands.
        p.   cm.
    Includes bibliographical references and index.
    ISBN 0–335–19639–X. — ISBN 0–335–19638–1 (pbk.)
    1. History—Study and teaching.   I. Title.
D16.25.H85   1996
907—dc20   95–47333
                                                                CIP

Typeset by Type Study, Scarborough
Printed in Great Britain by St Edmundsbury Press Ltd, Bury St Edmunds,
Suffolk

For Nicky

If history does not guarantee attitudes and aspirations it is a necessary if not a sufficient condition which might enable the making of informed choices. It cannot guarantee tolerance though it may give it some intellectual weapons. It cannot keep open closed minds though it may sometimes leave a nagging grain of doubt in them. Historical thinking is primarily mind-opening, not socializing

John Slater
'The politics of history teaching:
a humanity dehumanised?'
Special Professorial Lecture
London Institute of Education
1988

Contents

Preface

This book explores some ideas about the teaching and learning of history in schools. It looks at the way in which pupils learn history, the difficulties they encounter and some of the ways in which the subject is represented to them in classrooms. In doing so, the book draws eclectically on a variety of traditions in the recent development of, particularly, cultural and intellectual history, in the development of thinking about talk and writing in schools over the last decade and on the ways in which teachers and researchers in history education have been thinking about the nature of pupil learning.

Inevitably, in writing such a book I have been heavily reliant on discussions with students and colleagues. The book draws on some of the ideas I explored over five years of teaching at the University of East Anglia, and it would not have been written without the discussions I have been able to have with students, colleagues and schoolteachers. My own ideas have changed and developed considerably, but they would not have done so without these contacts. Amongst my students, I am particularly grateful to Jonathan Payne, Arthur Chapman, Peter Harris, Patrick Earnshaw, Helen Lugger, Mark Quinn and Indy Clark; their inputs into this text will be obvious to them. At the University of East Anglia, I was very grateful for long and always illuminating discussions with Beverley Labbett and Grant Bage. Edward Acton and Martin and Jennifer Tucker read substantial elements of the text and commented thoughtfully, helpfully and with controlled tact. Roy Barton has been able to introduce me to important parallel developments in science education, and to cast an outsider's eye on my work. Mike Hayhoe's guidance on ways of thinking about and supporting pupil writing was invaluable, and offered with great generosity of spirit. Susan Halliwell offered the insights of a modern languages specialist. The book was completed at Warwick University, and I thank colleagues there for their forbearance as I completed a text which must have seemed like a curious import to them. I have benefited from discussions with colleagues elsewhere, particularly with Martin Booth, Anna Pendry and Gwyn Prins. I was fortunate in being able to work with an efficient and sensitive editorial team at Open University Press, and would like to thank Shona Mullen, Pat Lee and Maureen Cox.

Most of all, though, this book is about classrooms, and I want to thank those teachers with whom I have been able to explore ideas about pupil learning and teacher strategies: I owe a debt of considerable gratitude over several years to Dan Archer, Ian Coulson, Lyn Gash, Shan George, Jim Harrison, Ian Hinde, Tim Lomas, Martin Oldfield, Martin Roberts and Colin Shephard. In spite of all this guidance, I alone am responsible for any shortcomings in the text.

This book was substantially written in the spring and summer of 1995, and without the forbearance and assistance, as ever, of Nicky, it would not have been written at all. As are all authors, I suspect that I was an uncomfortable presence while I tried to make the text, my understandings and my wordprocessor do things that they would not do. Nicky read elements of the book, and tidied up my text, as well as providing less tangible forms of support. Thanks to the intrusions of Emily, Harriet, Anna and Jessica, the book nearly was not written, but their interventions were always worth while in more ways than one, and they have taught me a great deal about how children think about history.

Chris Husbands
Reepham, Norfolk.

PART ONE

UNDERSTANDING HISTORY

'I will tell you,' I said, 'all about Robespierre.'
'I suppose,' said the man from the ministry, 'you mean that you will tell us all you know about Robespierre.'
'What he means,' said the party member, 'is that he will tell us what he wants us to think about Robespierre.'
'If you go on like this,' I replied, 'I won't tell you anything at all. I certainly don't intend to tell you all I know because a lot of it is of no interest to anybody. But as far as I can I'll tell you everything that I think you'd like to know and if I'm hiding anything you can always ask.'
'That's assuming, we know what we don't know,' said the man from the ministry.
'Well, its the best we can do. You've got to take something on trust and I'll undertake not to leave out anything I think you might think important even if I don't.'
　　　　N. Hampson (1974) *The Life and Opinions of Maximilian Robespierre*, p. 1. London: Duckworth.

The past exerts an endless fascination. We are interested in the past because we are interested in our roots, or because we are interested in the way the world around us has been shaped, or because we are intrigued by the 'otherness' of different people who lived at different times. These different motivations underpin learning about the past whether it is in the classroom, in the archive, or on a Sunday afternoon excursion. But what does 'learning history' mean? How do we organize information about the past into images of history?

Part One explores some of the 'building blocks' of learning about the past. This book is about the teaching and learning of history in schools, but in Chapter 1 I argue that learning about the past, however simple or sophisticated the learning, confronts some common and persistent problems. Some of the ways in which historical scholarship is changing in the light of recent developments in philosophy and social theory are examined.

In Chapters 2 to 5, I review some of these problems in more detail, exploring the relationships between classroom learning and thinking about the past. Chapter 2 looks at some of the problems of making sense of historical evidence, at asking questions of evidence and at organizing the answers which can be suggested to these questions. Chapter 3 looks at the relationship between the language we use to describe the past and the languages of historical actors. Chapter 4 looks at historical accounts, concentrating on the relationship between narrative stories and historical understanding. Finally Chapter 5 looks at the part which the exercise of the imagination plays in understanding history by considering the place of fictions in the accounts we give of the past.

These chapters can be read in any order, but they set out markers for the sort of classroom history developed in Part Two.

Chapter 1

Introduction: learning about the past

HAROLD BRIDGES LIBRARY
S. MARTIN'S COLLEGE
LANCASTER

How do we learn about the past? How do we communicate what we learn about the past to others? What is the connection between the way pupils learn about the past and the way historians make sense of the past? These questions prompt another: why do we learn (and teach) about the past?

The past, of course, once existed. Its remains are all around us: there are old buildings, archaeological sites, ruins and remains. There are books, documents and archives. There are representations of the past littered through our daily lives, in films, on television, in cartoons. Popular interest in the past has, perhaps, never been greater: people read about the past, they visit historic houses, they watch television histories. In schools pupils learn history; at home children and their parents talk, read or watch programmes about the past; in the library the historian probes aspects of the past. All of these activities, in some way or other, involve learning about the past, finding out what happened, what it was like, how it compares to our own lives.

Through its remains, and through the books and films which represent it, the past seems to be immediate and accessible. But our knowledge and understanding of the past will always be partial and incomplete. There are a number of reasons for this, some of them to do with the passing of time, others to do with the way people behaved, and yet others to do with our own relationship with the past. In the first place, there are many activities and ideas of people in the past to which we do not have access. Some of the evidence which once existed is now lost: Roman and Saxon settlement sites have been obliterated by succeeding generations; medieval manuscripts have been lost or destroyed; governments, among others, have deliberately destroyed written evidence. War, fire and decay have taken their toll. Other facets of life in the past were not recorded by contemporaries. We cannot find out, for example, much about the attitudes of medieval peasant women to their lives and their families or what slaves on slave plantations thought about their work, or about relationships between family members in the past. The evidence available for constructing accounts of the past is, then, partial and selective at best.

Where evidence does exist, it is often misleading. The assumptions and prejudices of authors or artists – often unspoken and unrevealed – confound the usefulness of much evidence as a window onto the past. Many of the archives which survive, for example, from European colonial administrations in Africa tell us more about their authors' presuppositions than about the African past. Apparently representational paintings from the sixteenth, seventeenth, eighteenth and nineteenth centuries were in practice highly stylized constructions deploying subtle and often arcane symbolism. Some evidence is simply fraudulent. Skilful historians can exploit the most unpromising and complex evidence in order to offer accounts of the past, but there is almost no historical evidence which can be taken at 'face value'.

These difficulties with evidence make up a large part of the challenge of understanding the past, but there are others. When we think about the past, we have our own assumptions, attitudes and questions which are different from those of people in the past. We use words, language and ideas, which are different from those of people in the past. The past, in L.P. Hartley's frequently quoted line in *The Go-between* 'is a foreign country. They do things differently there'. The questions we ask about the past, and the answers which we formulate differ from those of previous generations because we are different from them as much as because we have looked at different sources. Agreed historical procedures – careful, systematic readings of historical evidence, establishing its provenance, purpose and bias, cross-referencing different sources, and establishing what other historians have made of the evidence – can ameliorate some of the difficulties. Such procedures provide checks and balances on our ideas and interpretations but can never do so entirely. Mere invention can be distinguished from historical accounts by reference to the available evidence. Even so, accounts of the past are always interpretive and always open to dispute and question. The discipline of history is both less than the past (because not all of the past can be understood) and more than the past (because our accounts of the past are overlaid by our assumptions and presuppositions).[1]

As an academic discipline, history is an attempt to resolve these difficulties and to construct intellectually coherent accounts of the past which are consistent with the evidence. How far is this also true of history in schools? There are fundamental differences between the ways historians work and the ways pupils and teachers work. Where historians are engaged in an interpretive activity relating the current state of the discipline to new research findings, history teachers are largely concerned with their pupils' intellectual and personal development. Where historians are concerned with the archive, teachers are concerned with the classroom. There is an academic discipline called 'history', a school subject called 'history' and a widespread popular interest in 'history'. There is no reason why all these pursuits should have the same label, nor why the label should have the same meaning in different contexts.

We can, however, overemphasize distinctions between the different senses of history. If it is naïve to assume that the 11-year-old pupil in the classroom is engaged in a task which is comparable to the academic in the archive, it is nonetheless true that they are both engaged in constructing an interpretation of the past. The one may not 'model' the procedures of the other, but their different 'histories' have a common concern. Just as academic historians are concerned to develop understandings of the past whilst being aware of the limitations of historical method, so history teachers try to develop pupils' understandings of the past and of the limitations of historical understanding.

> Children, I have always taught you that history has its uses, its serious purpose. I always taught you the burden of our need to ask why. I taught you there is never any end to that question, because as I once defined it for you (yes, I confess a weakness for improvised definitions) history is that impossible thing: the attempt to give an account with

> incomplete knowledge, of actions themselves undertaken
> with incomplete knowledge. ⁞ . . . I taught you that by
> forever attempting to explain, we may come not to an
> Explanation but to a knowledge of the limits of our power
> to explain.
>
> > Graham Swift (1983) *Waterland*, pp. 181–2.
> > London: Heinemann.

History and teaching history

This book is concerned with the way in which we help pupils to understand the past, that is, to build up some intellectually coherent understanding of 'history'. It draws together three themes. The first of these is based on exploring the relations between the academic discipline of history and the teaching of history in schools at a time when both are undergoing change. There is a debate going on about the nature of history as a discipline, about its intellectual points of reference and about the knowledge which historians produce. Over the last thirty years, social and intellectual historians have explored new territories – the history of the family and population, of culture and belief, of sexuality and sexual attitudes, of groups hitherto 'hidden' from history: women, slaves, children, the mentally ill and so on. In their attempts to recover what Wachtel has memorably described as the 'vision of the vanquished', they have explored a wider variety of historical sources, examined previously studied sources in new ways and brought to bear on them insights and concepts culled from sociology, social theory and anthropology. Much of this work has resulted in a challenge not just to the findings of previous generations of historians, but to the concept of history as a unified academic discipline: historical accounts have been increasingly seen to be coloured by the concepts, questions and assumptions deployed by the historian.[2]

There has been a parallel controversy about school history, which originated in the 1960s and gathered pace in the 1980s and early 1990s. The controversy has involved a number of overlapping disagreements. There have been sharp debates about the content appropriate for the school history curriculum in a rapidly changing, multicultural society. There have been debates about the relative balance to be accorded to historical 'content' and historical 'skills' in the history classroom. There have been debates about the appropriate balance in classrooms between pupil investigation of historical problems and teacher exposition about the past. There have been debates about what sort of historical understanding can be attained, and how it should be assessed. All of these debates arise from fundamental dis-agreements about the nature and place of history in the school curriculum and society. All of them are significant debates, but they have tended to isolate school history from developments elsewhere in the discipline. Here we will consider whether a reappraisal of recent work in both school history and academic history helps us to resolve some of them.[3]

Language and learning

The second theme addressed by this book revolves around the relationship between language and learning. In the 1970s, there was widespread concern in schools about the need for teachers to think about 'language across the curriculum' and to encourage the use of language as a vehicle for learning in different ways in different areas of the curriculum. In the 1980s, this concern re-established itself as a concern for developing the quality of 'talk' and 'writing' across the curriculum. There is a real danger that language is a 'taken-for-granted' component of school life: that it becomes simply a mechanism by which teachers and pupils interact with each other rather than a vehicle for the exploration of ideas. The nature and quality of teacher talk and the nature and quality of pupil talk are of equal importance. Teachers ask questions about the past, they tell stories about the past, they respond to pupils' oral and written work. Pupils use words to recall information, to explore ideas, in large groups or in small groups. We need to specify clearly the ways we ask pupils to think about their work. Concern with language needs to translate also into the sorts of written work pupils are asked to undertake in learning about the past; there is a danger that written work in history becomes simply transactional, in re-sponse to questions, rather than a vehicle for the development of thinking about people in the past. This concern for language has, indeed, also been a feature of recent developments in the philosophy and historiography of academic history itself. Historians have exhibited sensitivity to language, to the language of historical actors and to the language of the historian, and in some cases have begun to reflect on the process of writing accounts of the past. In this book, then, we will explore the relationships between language and learning about the past. Reading, talking and writing are all overlapping aspects of history, and they are all intimately connected with the way we use and receive language.

Children, learning and history

The third theme which underpins the book is concerned with pupil thinking drawn from a wide range of research and development work in history and elsewhere. Thirty years ago, researchers, largely working within a Piagetian framework of cognitive psychology, were pessimistic about pupils' ability to build up informed understandings of the past. History was felt to be an academic discipline of ferocious difficulty which was beyond the capacity of most adolescent pupils for whom issues of historical evidence, motivation and ideas were too challenging. A variety of studies have undermined this view. Recent research has suggested that if appropriately taught and stimulated, pupils across the age and ability range are able to use ideas of subtlety and sophistication in thinking about the past. In this book, we draw together a range of research on pupil cognition and understanding in order to organize recent findings into a coherent model for the history classroom.

The organization of the book

These three themes run throughout the book, and are drawn on at different points. Part One of the book – Chapters 2 to 5 – explores some important ideas about the nature of history and the way in which we ask pupils to think about the past. Understanding the past demands an exercise of thinking on the part of pupils. We examine a variety of ways of making sense of the past: through interrogating the raw materials ('evidence') which are available to teachers and pupils, through deploying interpretive language about the past, through developing explanatory accounts ('making histories') and through exercising the imagination ('historical empathy'). At the root of all these chapters is the idea that the 'past' is not there, waiting for us to teach about it, but that understanding the past is something which pupils, historians and history teachers all engage in actively.

In Part Two – Chapters 6 to 9 – we set out the implications of the ideas explored earlier for the work we do in the classroom: the way we talk about the past, the way we organize pupils, the way we ask them to write and the way we make judgements on their work. In all of these chapters we investigate the relationships between the things teachers ask pupils to try to understand and the ways in which teachers ask them to work. The argument is for *integrative* and *holistic* ways of working in the classroom and to suggest that some versions of classroom history which disaggregated the subject into discrete skills may have been counterproductive in terms of the historical understandings they were intended to promote. Some teachers have drawn distinctions between the classroom 'processes' we ask pupils to engage in and the 'products' which emerge; here the emphasis is on the importance of *both* process and product.

The final chapter is more theoretical than the previous chapters, crystallizing ideas about the nature of the discipline in schools by referring briefly to some of the debates about school history. Drawing on the arguments advanced earlier, a wider intellectual framework for the discipline in schools is suggested.

This, then, is a book about *practice*. Whilst a wide range of thinking about the past and the way we make sense of it has been drawn on, the concern is to enable teachers – in whatever context – to think about their own practice. Teaching is a complex, confusing, busy and crowded activity. It occupies the minds of teachers at a wide variety of levels, and teachers, characteristically, are busy professionals. With this in mind, each chapter is deliberately quite short and tries to make its points clearly. For readers who want to go further, the notes at the end of each chapter are more detailed and pursue the sources of the arguments in more depth. They amplify the points made and provide full bibliographic references to the arguments advanced. Finally, each chapter uses boxes, quotations and diagrams to summarize the relationships between the ideas being explored.

Sources and acknowledgements

No book is 'invented', and this book more than most is dependent on the work of others, both friends and colleagues and others whose ideas I have encountered through their written work. I have tried to tie together some disparate threads of thinking which seem to me to say, together, powerful things about the way we might teach and learn history. Setting out some of important sources now serves two purposes. On the one hand it allows me to acknowledge frankly an intellectual debt which is traced in the endnotes to each chapter, but on the other it provides an opportunity for readers to go directly to my sources. It is worth saying, of course, that I have *used* these sources: the uses to which I have put the ideas I have worked up are not those which their authors ever imagined they might be put.

One source of the ideas in this book is to do with the way we think about and experience the past. Peter Burke's recent exploration of *History and Social Theory* is also reflected in these pages, particularly his lucid, and exceptionally well-informed exploration of developments in cultural and microhistory. I have also found extremely useful the arguments advanced in David Lowenthal's meticulously researched and wide-ranging book *The Past is a Foreign Country*. Similarly, I have drawn on a variety of work on the margins between history and cognate disciplines, particularly archaeology and anthropology. I find Michael Shanks' account of archaeology, *Experiencing the Past*, and the work of Jan Vansina on oral historiography extremely helpful.

A second source of ideas comes from recent work on the nature of language and creative thought in learning. Although this is a book about history, I want to acknowledge an enormous debt to a book about learning in another subject. I find the arguments about learning science in Clive Sutton's *Words, Science and Learning* both enormously fruitful for my own area of the curriculum and, which is just as important, expressed with a clarity and lucidity which can only be described as exemplary. Sutton's ideas are more generally explored in the collection he edited, *Communication in the Classroom*, and they derive in part from a wider concern to think about the role of language and communication in learning. Inevitably, I have also drawn on the work of Douglas Barnes, especially on *From Communication to Curriculum* and his more recent *School Writing*.

As a third source, I have drawn selectively on recent research into cognitive and curriculum development in history. Here, I have worked within the tradition of cognitive-psychological accounts of learning history exemplified by Martin Booth, Alaric Dickinson, Denis Shemilt, Peter Lee and Ros Ashby, and particularly by the outstanding work of Hilary Cooper on younger children's learning in history, especially in *History in the Early Years*.

> We do call the past, *as such*, into being by recollecting and by thinking historically, but we do this by disentangling it out of the present in which it actually exists.
>
> R.G. Collingwood (1926) Some perplexities about time, and an attempted solution. *Proceedings of the Aristotelian Society, New Series,* 26: 150.

Notes

1 On accounts of the nature of history, recent accounts are provided by John Tosh (1984) *The Pursuit of History*. London: Longman. See especially Chapter 1. See also Arthur Marwick (1970) *The Nature of History*. London: Macmillan. The relationship between the historian, the evidence and the past is explored by Gwyn Prins (1991) Oral history in P. Burke (ed.) *New Perspectives on Historical Writing*, pp. 114–39. Oxford: Polity Press. This is discussed in a more critical vein by Stephen Bann (1990) *The Inventions of History: essays on the representation of the past*. Manchester: University Press. See especially his essay on 'The inventions of history', pp. 1–11. A critical recent account is K. Jenkins (1996) *On 'What is History?'*. London: Routledge.

2 For a succinct and informative summary of recent developments in history, see P. Burke (1991a) Overture: the new history, its past and its future in P. Burke (ed.) op. cit., pp. 1–23. A more detailed account is provided for the development of social history by Adrian Wilson (1993) A critical portrait of social history in A. Wilson (ed.) *Rethinking Social History: English society 1570–1920 and its interpretation*. Manchester: Manchester University Press. See especially pp. 24–31 and 34–36.

3 On the controversies over school history, see: R. Samuel *et al.* (1990a) History the nation and the schools, *History Workshop Journal*, 29: 92–133

and R. Samuel *et al.* (1990b) History the nation and the schools, *History Workshop Journal*, 30: 75–128; C. Husbands and A. Pendry (1992) *Whose History? School History and the National Curriculum*. History Education Group: University of East Anglia; and C. Husbands (1992b) Facing the facts: history in schools and the curriculum in P. Black (ed.) *Education: Putting the Record Straight*. Stafford: Network Educational Press.

Chapter 2

Understanding the past: evidence and questions

One way to start thinking about how we build up understandings of the past in the classroom is to consider the raw materials which are available. These raw materials or 'relics' are not, in themselves, 'history', or 'the past', but they provide one basis for constructing historical knowledge. In one sense, the past is dead. Being past, the experiences of people in earlier times can only be recovered through analysis based on the relics they have left behind, through the physical, material and documentary remains available to us, even though such might be misleading or inaccurate. But in another sense, of course, the past is not dead at all: it exists through the ways in which *we* understand the past, and in the personal, cultural and intellectual inheritance we each have. The past is constructed through our interpretations, which in turn derive from the questions we think it important to ask about relics of the past. Indeed, until we begin to ask questions about the relics we have, they are not, in any useful sense, evidence at all. The development of historical understanding is always the result of an active dialogue between ourselves, in the present, and the evidence in whatever form which the past has left behind.

History is difficult because of the ambiguous relationships between our interests, the relics we have, or might find, the gaps, elisions and distortions which the relics contain, and of course the past which generated the relics. Unless we examine the historical evidence, we cannot answer with confidence the question 'How do we know this happened?' In some cases, historical problems arise because there are too many relics to be

Figure 2.1   Evidence, questioning and interpreting history.

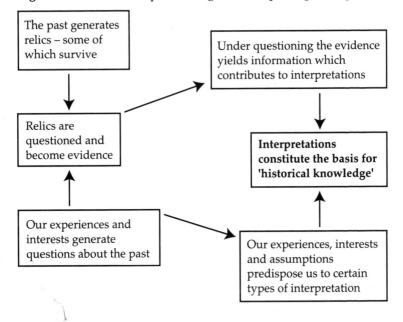

consulted so that the historian is forced to select from what remains; in others they arise because there are scarcely any surviving relics. For historians of the twentieth century, the sheer scale of Churchill's papers, or the archives relating to the Treaty of Versailles make selection necessary; by contrast, what we can attempt to understand about life in the Neolithic Revolution depends on the interpretation of very few archaeological sites, looked at in different ways. In some cases, problems arise because the relics, though plentiful, can provide information on the perspectives of only an unrepresentative sample of the historical actors – the besetting problem, for example, of historians of the imperial encounter in nineteenth century Africa where the *written* record tells only the tale of the Europeans, or, similarly, in sixteenth century central America; in others, problems arise because the relics are internally inconsistent and contradictory. In yet other cases, disputes arise from the significance which may be attributed to one piece of evidence set against another, or, more intriguingly, the significance of what survives set against what may or may not have survived: we cannot, for example, be sure about the extent to which the Romans introduced new agricultural practices into Britain be-cause no Roman field patterns have – as yet – been identified. The accounts historians offer of the past are themselves relics: they are both useful in defining the ways in which others have looked at the past and a reminder that historians' ideas are always powerfully affected by the time at which they worked. For all of these reasons and more, the construction of historical under-standings and historical knowledge is always provisional. The relationship between what we want to know and what the surviving relics are able to tell us is taut and problematic (Figure 2.1). The deployment of historical relics in the service of historical understanding is, for historians of whatever age, intellectually forbidding.[1]

Pupils and historical evidence

The issues surrounding historical evidence are so complex that some cognitive psychologists working in the tradition estab-lished by the work of Jean Piaget have argued that the use of such evidence in the classroom is too difficult for pupils. Piaget suggested that pupils' intellectual development proceeds through four 'stages'. Only at the third stage of 'concrete operations' – from about the age of 7 years – do elements of logical and deductive reasoning appear, manifested in thinking about the immediate, the contemporary and the observable. At the fourth stage from about the age of 11 years, pupils develop 'formal operational thought', characterized by the capacity to deal with propositions and hypotheses and to make deductions. As a result, Piagetian psychologists argued that adolescent and pre-adolescent pupils had only a limited capacity for making inferences from evidence, for testing evidential hypotheses and for thinking about past experiences in abstract ways. The task of constructing accounts of the past from evidential materials was said to depend on the capacity for formal operational thinking which few pupils demonstrated. If pupils had any capacity for learning about history, it could be defined at best as the ability to accumulate 'facts' about the past, since more complex, abstract relationships are simply beyond most pupils.

The Piagetian view of pupils' capacities appears to be no longer tenable; a wide range of research has shown that pupils can use historical evidence to develop and test hypotheses about the past providing that such evidence is presented to them appropriately.[2] Such research has buttressed the emphasis placed on the use of evidence in history teaching. Most teachers of history in schools would now argue that if evidence is the 'basis of the discipline' then the development of 'historical skills' in the use of evidence is an essential prerequisite of accumulating information about and understanding of the past.[3] The use of historical sources – visual, written, oral, physical and so on – has become a staple of classroom history over the last twenty-five years.

Evidence and 'historical' thinking in the classroom

Teachers have used two general justifications for placing evidence at the centre of work in the history classroom. The first is to do with *general arguments about the role of history in the curriculum*. In these arguments, history is an evidence-processing activity which plays an essential part in the preparation of pupils for the demands of life outside and beyond school, where they will be confronted with a mass of information, much of it conflicting and much of it advanced by advocates of particular political or commercial persuasions. The intellectual discipline of collecting, processing and rigorously analysing historical evidence is, then, one of the ways in which teachers in schools prepare pupils for analysing information they will be presented with later.

The second and more specific justification is to do with the *nature of history as a discipline*. Historians only have access to the past via its remains: we cannot, therefore, acquire any historical understandings without addressing historical evidence. Historical evidence is not simply the basis for information-processing activities, it is also an avenue of enquiry into the historicity of the past, into exploring the language, and the meanings which language had for participants. This is as true of the collection of information as it is of the interrogation of viewpoints about the historical past: questions about whether Henry VIII was a 'tyrant', or about the religious motivations of Oliver Cromwell are ultimately soluble by recourse to primary evidence. In these justifications for using evidence in the teaching of history, the use of evidence is not an optional 'extra' but an essential component in developing pupils' historical understanding, even though the challenge is formidable. Asking and answering questions of historical evidence is a key element of learning history.

Where such justifications have been weaker is in seeing school history as largely concerned with primary evidence, so that pupils come to historical sources without a sense of the way in which others have already made sense of them. Some academic historians remain very sceptical. For at least one eminent historian: 'Any thought that children can usefully analyse or evaluate the nature of the evidence seems to me to be seriously mistaken.'[4] The charge is that it is naïve to suppose that we can consider the 'pupil as historian' in the classroom. The length, the conceptual and linguistic difficulties of many sources, and in some cases their sheer boredom, make it impossible for pupils to make any realistic appraisal of their significance. The teacher's normal tactic, of editing, cutting, or pre-selecting evidence upon which pupils will practice the 'historical skills' often results in activities which can scarcely be dignified with the label 'history', and, in many cases, the 'skills' themselves operate at a lamentably low level. A preoccupation with primary historical evidence underplays the importance of secondary accounts which provide the framework within which questions are posed and answers developed: no historian would embark on a historical investigation without considering what other historians had written. Finally, the focus on developing the 'skills of the historian' neglects the extent to which history is a form of public knowledge: the development of 'evidential skills' in effect distracts attention from historical content. In these senses, the widespread use of historical evidence in the classroom is said to undermine the development of effective historical understanding.

The starting point for most teachers in thinking about the ways pupils appear to understand historical evidence has been, in some form, Benjamin Bloom's *A Taxonomy of Educational Objectives*. Essentially, Bloom suggests that we cannot value or judge something until we know and understand the facts, apply them, take them apart and put them together in ways which produce new perspectives. Bloom's taxonomy has been enormously influential in shaping evidence-based work. It has provided a model which allows teachers to develop pupil thinking through a hierarchy of questions from simple to complex, from comprehension/extraction to evaluation, from comprehension to inference, from the focus on a single source to the synthesis of numerous sources, from the particular to the general. Hierarchies like this have real value in helping to shape the way we think about pupil learning, and, in England they have been influential in the Schools' Council History Project, in the GCSE and in the National Curriculum. But they also create some difficulties for teachers. 'Simple' recall questions may be dull or boring; difficult 'evaluation' questions may be more lively, and, in some cases, working with complex historical sources such as some paintings, more accessible. Bloom's taxonomy is a way of looking at knowledge, not a structure for teaching. The overuse of the taxonomy as a basis for questioning implies an assumption that pupil learning itself proceeds through a linear progression which is independent of context: it assumes that pupils can develop 'evidence skills' which are independent of the evidence being studied: again, the significance of the context of evidence, of the ways others have made sense of it, is underplayed.[5]

Evidence and types of thinking

Is it possible to resolve these difficulties about the use of evidence in history teaching? Let us take an artefact, here a Greek pot (Figure 2.2). The Greek pot is a relic of Ancient Greek society. What are the sorts of historical question which we can pose about the Greek pot? How old is it? What is it made of? How was the decoration applied? Is it typical of pots of its period? What was it used for when it was made? What does the fact that we encounter it now in a museum tell us about the Greeks and about ourselves? How significant is it that we encounter it in a museum in London, or on a cheap postcard? Is it attractive? What have other historians already told us about such artefacts? Is there broad consensus or disagreement about such artefacts?

In principle, the range of questions which the pot stimulates is probably limitless. It is only through asking these questions that the pot itself 'gains' meaning: the questions generate the identity of the pot as a piece of 'evidence' which can yield 'information'. Some of the questions we might pose can be asked from the internal evidence of the pot itself; others would depend on consulting other sources – perhaps other pots – and yet others would depend on bringing to the pot some knowledge about

Figure 2.2 Black-figured neck-amphora showing Herakles breaking off one of the antlers of the Keryneian deer. Copyright The Trustees of the British Museum.

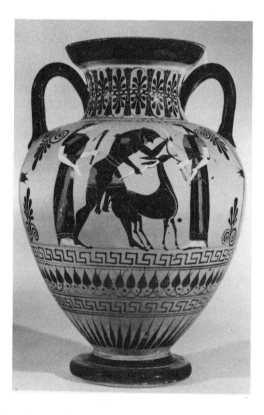

Greek society derived from historians' accounts in monographs, textbooks and so on. We might develop questions about issues on which the pot unwittingly fails to inform us, about issues in the past on which we have little evidence but which contemporary historians are interested: about, for example, the role of women in Greek society.

The 'evidence' can be addressed in a wide variety of ways. The way in which teachers select, from this limitless range of questions about the Greek pot, those they will ask in the classroom will depend on a number of factors, and not least of these is the nature of the historical enquiry on which they are embarked. The questions will be different if the concern is with the nature of technological processes and change in an ancient society, or the way in which Athenian society was organized.

Over and above these concerns are a second set. Amongst the questions posed above, there are questions which make generically different demands on the learner in order to advance a response: in this way, Bloom's taxonomy is useful but its usefulness is limited. It is not that some of the questions are more difficult than others, though some clearly *are* more difficult than others, but that the construction of interpretations of the pot through questioning is a multidimensional activity: just as there are an infinite variety of questions which could be posed about the Greek pot, so there are an infinite variety of combinations of questions which could be asked about the pot. To ask effective questions is less a matter of constructing a hierarchy of questions than about specifying the sorts of thinking about the pot which our questions are intended to promote. For this reason, we might begin to organize the questions we want to ask in terms of the nature of the thinking which we ask pupils to undertake in answering them. This is a different sort of approach to the study of evidence from that which we looked at earlier: it involves considering the sort of learning and the sort of thinking we want pupils to undertake.

Consider a second relic, this time a written historical source. The example is drawn from the text of a broadsheet circulating in London in 1650.

> About 10 in the morning the King was brought from St James's walking on foot through the Park, with a regiment of foot, part before, and part behind him with colours flying, drums beating . . . The Scaffold was hung around with black and the floor covered with black and the Axe and the block hid in the middle of the Scaffold. There were divers companies of Foot and Troops of Horse placed on the one side of the Scaffold towards Charing Cross and the multitudes of People that came to be spectators very great. The King being come upon the scaffold look'd very earnestly on the Block and asked Col Hacker if there were

no higher; and then spake thus (directing his speech chiefly to Col Tomlinson):

'All the World knows that I never did begin a war with the two Houses of Parliament, for I do believe that ill instruments between them and me has been the chief cause of all this bloodshed . . . I have forgiven all the world and even those in particular that have been the chief causers of my death. . . . For the people; And truly I desire their liberty and freedom as much as anybody whomsoever, but I must tell you that their liberty and freedom consists in having of government those laws by which their life and their goods may be most their own. It is not for having a share in government that is pertaining to them; A subject and a sovereign are clean different things, and therefore until you do put the people in that liberty as I say certainly they will never enjoy themselves. Sir it was for this I am come here. If I would have given way to an arbitrary way for to have all laws changed according to the power of the Sword, I needed not to have come here and therefore I tell you . . . that I am the martyr of the people. . .'

Then the King turning to Dr Juxon said, 'I have a good cause and a gracious God on my side.'

From *King Charles: His Speech* made upon the Scaffold at Whitehall Gate (1649).

The text here, as with most historical texts is a complex one: presented as a description of a historical event (the execution of Charles I) with a quotation of a historical actor (the about-to-be-executed king), the text is rather a Royalist justification for the king's stance during the 1640s and an early shot in the much longer struggle over the appropriate way in which to commemorate the king. It is, then, simultaneously a window which allows us to address the events of the 30 January 1649 and a curtain which obscures those events: we cannot know whether this is what Charles *said*, and *a priori* it appears unlikely. Again it is possible to generate any number of questions about this text: Are these the words of the king? Is this a reliable account of the moments before the execution? What have historians told us about the popular reaction to the execution of the king? Some of the questions might be concerned with the extraction of literal meanings from the text, others with inferred meanings by cross-referencing the text to other materials in order to relate the text to the events it describes, and yet others to the subtext. Although this is an extract from a longer document, and presented out of context, studying this text provides a basis for developing some understanding. This source, an apparently evocative description of the execution of the king is primarily accessible not as a piece of historical reportage but as a starting point for thinking about the event, for generating a dialogue between learners and the text. Again, these questions can be organized in terms of the nature of the thinking pupils undertake in answering them: the evidence provides the basis for the construction of a wide range of potential understandings.

Looking at single relics can be useful for both teachers and learners. It can be a way of establishing some canons of historical method (prompting questions about the historical context, clarifying points of detail, establishing issues such as authenticity, purpose, reliability, evaluating the usefulness of a particular item for a given enquiry and so on). It can also be helpful as a way of framing some of the wider issues about the way in which we can develop inferences or test hypotheses using historical evidence.

In practice, however, historical understanding is rarely built on the basis of single evidential relics. In most cases, interpretations depend on encountering relics in conjunction with each other: making comparisons, testing ideas and hypotheses, synthesizing diverse material and so on. We want the outcome of the encounter with evidence for pupils to be some understanding or interpretation of the past based on ideas which they develop from the collection of sources they have reviewed. The culmination, or purpose, of our work is for pupils to construct an interpretation in response to an enquiry about the past.

The previous paragraph used a variety of words to describe the activities which pupils might undertake when dealing with evidence, inference, interpretation, synthesis and so on. All the words described different types of thinking which evidence might support. In a highly sensitive analysis of questioning, Juliana Saxton and Norah Morgan point out that 'thinking' itself is a useful shorthand term for a wide range of different activities (see Table 2.1). As Saxton and Morgan observe, some of these

Table 2.1 Descriptions of thinking (from Juliana Saxton and Norah Morgan (1994) *Asking Better Questions*. London: Drake Publishing)

Connecting	Contrasting	Rehearsing	Inducing
Arguing	Projecting	Testing	Approximating
Convincing	Questioning	Clarifying	Selecting
Generating	Reconciling	Reflecting	Deducing
Analysing	Suspending	Judging	Generalising
Capitulating	Wondering	Disrupting	Alluding
Relating	Rejecting	Co-operating	Solving
Composing	Hazarding	Synchronising	Matching
Retracting	Modifying	Harmonising	Probing
Associating	Including	Speculating	Eliciting
Sequencing	Inventing	Contradicting	Soliciting
Suggesting	Extending	Assimilating	Recalling
Sorting	Accommodating	Empathising	Calculating
Imagining	Proving	Compromising	Formulating
Comparing	Hypothesising	Refuting	Valuing
Intuiting	Refining	Internalising	Abstracting
	Predicting	Improving	

words are near synonyms (e.g. 'arguing' and 'convincing'), but others describe quite different activities. 'Reflecting' is quite different from 'recalling'; 'speculating' different from 'comparing'; 'refining' different from 'formulating'. Some of the words describe activities which in themselves are more relevant in some curriculum areas than in others, that is, in some areas of a teacher's work more than in others. Saxton and Morgan argue that by focusing on types of thinking in this way we avoid artificial boundaries which constrain work with pupils, between 'knowledge' and 'understanding', between 'reflection' and 'analysis'. They insist that the important focus is on the relationship between the teacher, the learner, and the material being taught, on the way learners *think* about what they are asked to do.[6]

How do we begin to sort these different words into a serviceable teaching tool? If we look at teaching and learning in this way, then teachers need to be clear about the sorts of thinking which they are attempting to generate so that questions can develop, rather than confuse that thinking. The list in Table

Table 2.2 A simple model for developing types of thinking about evidence

Questions which elicit information: accretion	Questions which elicit reflection: judgemental	Questions which elicit understanding	
		Divergent	Convergent
These questions require facts, precise recall, recognition or observation. They are close questions in that they seek a single correct answer. • What is it made from? • What is happening to the king in this picture?	These questions provide personal [perhaps unique] answers. They require choice and evaluation and involve the formulation of an opinion or belief. • Should we spend money on preserving paintings like this one? • Was the author of this letter justified to believe that . . .?	These questions allow for more than one possible right answer. They demand imaginative thinking, formulating an hypothesis and the ability to solve problems. Prediction, inference and reconstruction might be needed. • How could the design of this object be improved? • What interpretations of these events can you suggest using these items?	These seek the most appropriate or best answer. They focus on what is already known or perceived. They might require explanations, interpretations, comparisons or interrelationships. • What was this object used for? • Why was this letter written? • How could you make it work? • Does the evidence suggest that it is right to suppose that?

2.1 is too long to be really useful in the classroom. We need a simpler model to begin to support the generation of thinking in the classroom. Saxton and Morgan outline three general purposes of classroom question:

- Questions which elicit information (recalling, remembering, suggesting implications).
- Questions which elicit understanding . Such questions may be either *divergent* (promoting expression of attitudes, reasoning) or *convergent* (making connections, demanding inference and interpretation).
- Questions which elicit reflection (judging, creating, reasoning).

Table 2.2 adapts the Saxton and Morgan model of thinking about questions to suggest a general set of approaches to thinking about historical evidence. None of these sorts of thinking which the table establishes is 'harder' or 'easier' than any other type; they are simply different modes of thinking about evidence in relation to the historical past; they call for different sorts of thinking on the part of the learner, and they can be deployed by teachers and learners in ways which support different enquiries.

Evidence and 'constructing' the past

The classification in Table 2.2 is probably not exclusive: there are other categories of thinking, other types of question which, say, the Greek pot or the Royalist broadsheet, could generate in different historical enquiries. But there are some important consequences of the approach which has been sketched. The first is to do with the nature of historical enquiry in the classroom. 'Hierarchies' of questions have been deployed as a way of 'moving' pupils towards 'higher' levels of historical understanding. However, on this model, higher levels are not in themselves developed through particular types of question or cognitive demands. Rather pupil understanding is developed via the type of thinking which questions are intended to support, and this places obvious obligations on the teacher in developing approaches to evidence which engage the learner's attention, feelings and interests to generate understandings.

A second consequence of this approach is to do with the sorts of response to the past which evidence makes possible. A pupil holds a piece of pottery, or reads a report of an archaeological dig. A pupil reads a narrative of the execution of King Charles I and looks at a print of the execution published some months later. A pupil reads a history textbook. Do they bring the past home to pupils? Are they signs, traces of the past? The print, the pot, the census return, the textbook *describing* the execution of the king cannot be reduced to definitive meanings. The relics are both less than the past – because they are fragmentary survivals of it – and more than the past because they need to be given meanings by ourselves and our pupils. There is always more in the evidence than questioning and interpretation can address. The past is not 'present' within the evidence, giving it an identity: we might see in the pot colours which remind us of decorations at home or posters in the street, or shapes in the patterns which call to mind cartoon characters. The description of the execution makes us angry, sad, regretful. The evidence is the basis for something in ourselves rather than being something simply 'from the past': it does not have a clear identity. In this, the past itself is not what is generating the meaning. The meaning is generated through thought processes which enable meanings to be conferred on the past. The meanings of relics, or the evidence, of the survivals, are social and personal.

This concern with pupil thinking is a reminder that the place of historical evidence in the classroom is subtly different from its place in the work of historians. Unlike historians, school pupils will not claim to generate 'new' public knowledge from the study of (selected) historical evidence; they will generate new private understandings. Evidence has a place in historical work in the classroom not because it thereby makes classroom history 'authentic', nor because it 'models' the activity of the historian, but because of the sorts of thinking it supports and the sorts of learning it makes possible.[7] The Greek pot and the broadsheet have a place in the history classroom as a basis for pupil thinking about the past, and equally, pieces of evidence which are themselves interpretations of that past have a place in the classroom. The key is the thinking which the evidence generates. For teachers, the task is about using evidence to develop types of thinking about the past. The evidence base of history provides us with a web of materials which makes possible the construction of historical understandings.

Notes

1 On the nature of 'evidence' in the work of the historian, the most accessible account remains J.H. Hexter (1972) *The History Primer*. London: Penguin. See especially Chapter 3, pp. 84–94. Hexter's argument about the importance of the historian's 'second record' in making sense of the evidence is developed by J. Tosh (1984) *The Pursuit of History*. Harlow: Longman. See especially pp. 48–72: Tosh emphasizes the 'flair for turning old sources to new uses'. The importance of 'historical logic', or the 'work of minds trained in a discipline of attentive disbelief' is addressed by E.P. Thompson (1978) *The Poverty of Theory*, pp. 220–1. London: Merlin.

2 On pupil ability to construct understandings using evidence, the central texts in dismantling the Piagetian view are those by Martin Booth and Hilary Cooper. Booth demonstrated that 15-year-old pupils were able to think 'adductively' about historical evidence: thinking which went beyond the evidence given to 'inferred qualities or ideas'. This thinking was 'adventurous, creative and accurately imaginative . . . the hallmarks of historical thought'. Booth concluded that 'fourteen to sixteen year old pupils are perfectly capable of construing the past in a genuinely historical manner'. See M.B. Booth (1993) *The Teaching and Learning of History: a British Perspective*, pp. 8–9. Göteborgs Universitet: Projektet Europa och Läroboken. H. Cooper (1992) *The Teaching of History*. London: David Fulton, sets out the limitations of Piagetian experimental conclusions to show that appropriate, open-ended teaching methodologies allow pupils to think inductively about evidence in a historical way. See also P. Harnett (1993) Identifying progression in children's understanding: the use of visual materials to assess primary school children's learning in history. *Cambridge Journal of Education*, 23(2): 137–54, especially p. 149: 'children need to develop skills in interpreting sources and in using them as evidence to support their conclusions . . . [by] asking questions'.

3 On the use of evidence in the classroom, see John Fines (1994) Evidence: the basis of the discipline? in H. Bourdillon (ed.) *Teaching History*, pp. 122–6. London: Routledge for the Open University; also HMI (1985) *History in the Primary and Secondary Years*, pp. 2–3, 19. London: HMSO offers general support for the second justification; the first is suggested on p. 19. Fines argues that 'using source-material and tackling the problems of evidence gives a feeling of reality which second-hand history can rarely give'. A succinct and thoughtful general discussion of the place of evidence in the history classroom remains A.K. Dickinson, A. Gard and P.J. Lee (1978) Evidence in history and the classroom in A.K. Dickinson and P.J. Lee (eds) *History Teaching and Historical Understanding*, pp. 1–17. London: Heinemann. They propose a critique of some of Fines' direct assumptions about

evidence but conclude by arguing that 'because of the relationship between evidence and historical knowledge, the gradual development of children's historical understanding must go hand in hand with the acquisition of knowledge of the historical context which produced that evidence'.

4 On critiques of evidence-based approaches, the charge has been led by G.R. Elton and, more recently, Robert Skidelsky. See G.R. Elton (1970) What sort of history should we teach? in M. Ballard (ed.) *New Movements in the Study and Teaching of History*. London: Temple Smith. Also, R. Skidelsky (1988a) A question of values. *Times Educational Supplement*, 27 May 1988. From a quite different ideological position, Keith Jenkins argues that the use of historical evidence in the classroom results in a sleight of hand whereby 'the past' is supplanted as a target of study by 'the sources', some ('primary') are seen to be of higher value than others; in consequence, the sense of history as an arena of discourse about experience is denied. See K. Jenkins (1991) *Rethinking History*, pp. 47–52. London: Routledge.

5 On 'hierarchical taxonomies' of pupil understanding of evidence, the starting point is B.S. Bloom (1956) *A Taxonomy of Educational Objectives. I.* London: Longman. Bloom's influence on history teaching was largely through J.B. Coltham and J. Fines (1970) *Educational Objectives for the Study of History*. London: Historical Association. Gard and Lee show that the Coltham and Fines' approach both devalues the place of *understanding* in history and elevates a view of history organized around 'behavioural objectives'. See A. Gard and P.J. Lee (1978) 'Educational objectives for the study of history' reconsidered in A.K. Dickinson and P.J. Lee (eds) op. cit., pp. 21–38, especially pp. 36–8. The influence of Bloom, Coltham and Fines is particularly strong on D. Gunning (1978) *The Teaching of History*. London: Croom Helm, and appears to have been an influence on the Schools' Council History Project: see Schools' Council (1976) *A New Look at History*, pp. 8 [note 4] and 11 [note 5]. Through this route, the emphasis on cognitive development through objectives was influential on both GCSE and the National Curriculum. See R. Medley and C. White (1991) Assessing the national curriculum: lessons from assessing history. *Curriculum Journal*, 3, 1.

6 On questions and thinking, see Juliana Saxton and Norah Morgan (1994) *Asking Better Questions*. London: Drake Publishing. This was originally published under the 1991 title *Teaching Questioning and Learning*. London: Routledge. See especially pp. 9–17. The table of types of thinking was originally published by New South Wales Department of Education in 1978. I owe a great deal to discussions of questioning with Lyn Gash and Susan Halliwell.

7 On evidence and classroom learning, the position is stated with some precision, and considerable hesitation by Dickinson, Gard and Lee: 'it

is possible to speak of children learning some of the . . . methods of the historian through limited practice with source material. . . . It *may* be a necessary prerequisite of learning history that certain activities in certain respects conflicting with the strict canons of professional practice occur in schools'. See A.K. Dickinson, A. Gard and P.J. Lee (1978) op. cit., p. 14. Keith Jenkins, op. cit., pp. 47–52 (in an argument with which I otherwise sympathize) and G.R. Elton, op cit, for different reasons understate this distinction. S. Wineburg (1991) On the reading of historical texts: notes on the breach between School and Academy. *American Education Research Journal*, 28(3): 499–515, argues that academic historians and high-school pupils think in fundamentally different ways about the evidence in front of them, but that appropriately designed tasks can introduce the latter to the *modus operandi* of the former.

HAROLD BRIDGES LIBRARY
S. MARTIN'S COLLEGE
LANCASTER

Chapter 3

Understanding the past: language and change

A second way to appreciate the way in which we construct knowledge about the past is to consider the sorts of language we have
to convey historical ideas and historical concepts. Historians and
history teachers themselves have been divided about the linguistic difficulty of history; some argue that history is riven with
linguistic difficulties of distinctive and formidable complexity
which render the accumulation of valid historical understandings
problematic for many students. From this perspective, historical
understanding is not possible without a command of historical
vocabulary. Others argue that history poses no specialist language since it is a subject closely related to human experience; the
language register of history is simply 'intellectual lumber' which
the student picks up along the way since the language is always
encountered in specific historical contexts which support the
generation of meanings. In this chapter, we will explore some of
the different ways in which historical language features in the development of understandings of the past.

Historical language, of course, has several quite distinct components; it refers to the ways in which we make sense of how
people in the past expressed their actions, thoughts and beliefs,
but it also refers to the ways in which historians have tried to describe the historical processes which those people experienced
and shaped (Figure 3.1). This in turn involves considering both
the way historians use difficult, abstract concepts and the way in
which they use what I want to call the *organizing principles* of the
subject. By this I mean the ideas of causation, similarity, difference, continuity and so on which we draw on to give shape,
meaning and structure to our interpretations of the past.

Figure 3.1 Types of historical language.

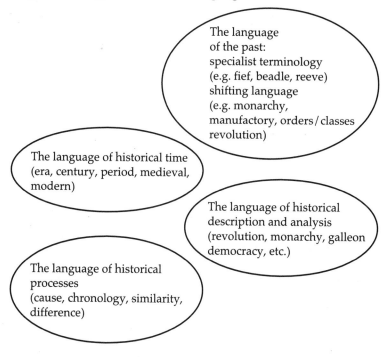

Words from the past

The language of history – that is, the language of past peoples and societies – is not the language of the present. This is obviously true when we are attempting to describe societies linguistically different from our own, such as the Ancient Greeks or Romans, or the Incas or Aztecs, but it is equally true of English-speakers of even the quite recent past. When people in the fifteenth or early sixteenth centuries spoke of a 'gentleman', they meant something quite different from the modern, generic meaning of the term. 'Villain' has a clear modern meaning, which was established by the sixteenth century, but its derivation was from a technical medieval meaning. More typical, perhaps, are words which have changed their meaning substantially over time and in different ways, particularly abstract words. An important, and obvious example is the word 'class'. Although the word had a strict classical meaning, it was common as a general word for a group or division, though without modern social implications, from the later seventeenth century. The modern sense of class, with relatively fixed names for particular classes, was a feature of the later eighteenth and particularly nineteenth centuries. Of course, most pupils immediately identify with a quite different, *school* use of the word.

'Revolution' is another word which now has a series of different meanings in different, though overlapping contexts. Its nineteenth century, predominantly political meaning (the French Revolution) extends to economic, and, increasingly, social meanings: the Neolithic Revolution, the Agrarian Revolution, the Industrial Revolution. Its historical origins were quite different. Textbooks refer to its derivation from the Latin, *revolvere*, to revolve, and this was its earliest English meaning: 'in whiche the other Planetes, as well as the Sonne do finyshe their revolucion and course according to their true tyme'. The political sense of the word gained in strength throughout the seventeenth century, particularly after the events of 1688, though not the events of 1640–60. It was the French Revolution at the end of the eighteenth century which fixed the modern political sense of the word, but during the nineteenth century the development of the factory system and the new industrial technology which accompanied it was called, by analogy and coincidence in time with the French Revolution, the Industrial Revolution. In the twentieth century, the political sense began to weaken. Rapid social or economic change, perhaps by analogy with the Industrial Revolution increasingly, and often indiscriminately, attracted the label 'revolution': hence the 'sexual revolution', the 'technological revolution', the 'communications revolution'. In these cases, the pattern of change in meaning is part of the process of historical change which we are trying to understand: the way in which contemporaries began to define revolution, the way in which a language of class emerged is part of the way in which the historical processes which gave rise to the language were formed.[1]

One of the consequences of this characteristic of historical language, which makes the learning of history fraught with difficulty, is that the language being used has multiple meanings. Learners and teachers construe meanings in different ways. It is not that the language of history is unfamiliar to the learner but that the learner already attaches different meanings to the language. This was particularly the case with revolution and with class. Douglas Barnes provides a different, though parallel instance of the ways in which the historical context of language provides a barrier to learning. A teacher discusses buildings in a medieval village with a class of 12-year-old pupils:

Teacher: There's another building there, not a house, but what?
Pupil: A mill.
Teacher: A mill, a mill. We have lots of mills in this area. This isn't the sort of mill we have around here. What goes on in this mill?
Pupil: Sir, water.
Teacher: Pardon?
Pupil: Water . . . for washing.
Teacher: Washing? [Laughter] . . . It's not a washing mill. Yes, D—.
Pupil: Is it a power house?
Teacher: A power house for what?
Pupil: Electricity.

Barnes comments that the pupils interpret what the teacher says through what they already know. They cannot set the word 'mill' into its (historical) context because they do not distinguish between (present-day) meanings of mill and (medieval) meanings of the word.[2] Similar, and more complex problems are posed by words which at first sight seem to have retained their historical meaning. 'King' is a good example. Historians use the word to communicate something more abstract than the person of a king; they frequently use it as a synonym for the office of the monarch, or, more abstractly, for the concept of 'kingship'. Now this is an exceptionally difficult idea, because kingship and the offices and actions of kings are constantly shifting. The late medieval monarchy, the personalized state of Henry VIII, the divine right of James I and Charles I and the constitutional monarchy of the eighteenth century were all historically different variants of monarchy. Finally, each of these thumbnail historical characterizations of monarchy has further variations: the concept of divine right differed between seventeenth century England and eighteenth century France. But it is difficult for learners to locate any of these different variants of monarchy against each other where they are unable to 'calibrate' them against the nature of monarchy today. For many adolescent pupils, the monarch remains the source of authority in modern Britain. In other words, learning about the concept of kingship frequently involves two sets of simultaneous learning: learning about power and its distribution in past societies and learning about power and its distribution in modern society. The former cannot be given real meaning until pupils have some more contemporary knowledge against which to calibrate their historical understandings. In this instance, the linguistic and contextual problems of learning about the past are overlapping.

Historians and language

The nature of language, as seen from the above discussion, can be part of the process of building up historical understandings of the past. However, historians frequently use language in ways which are far from literal or immediately straightforward, or in ways which create difficulties for learners. As Edwards has pointed out, these characteristics of history drag the subject always towards higher levels of abstraction in its use of language. Talk about the past is full of metaphor, generalization and concepts which we use in often shifting ways. One example is the way in which historians use specific names as labels for larger sets of ideas.[3] The word 'Victorian' is an important, and problematic example. At its simplest, it refers to a historical period in the United Kingdom between 1837 and 1901. But historians use the word with both a narrower and wider meaning, and it has a popular currency too: Victorian terraced housing, Victorian 'style', the 'Victorians' (people born during Queen Victoria's reign? people active during Queen Victoria's reign? people who evidence a particular set of behaviours and beliefs?), or, most contentious of all, perhaps, 'Victorian values' and so on. So the development of understanding the ideas which underpin the language becomes extremely difficult because the 'historical' language is being used in a particularly flexible way. If Victorian is an obvious, and particularly slippery example, others work in similar ways. Some examples are particularly non-literal in nature: the 'Black Death', the 'Scramble for Africa', the 'Triangular Trade'.

All of these are examples of difficulties which arise from the use of specific vocabulary, but historians also deploy a sophisticated 'grammar' of history.[4] The simple past tense of 'She *was* queen', or 'Columbus *discovered* America' is relatively straightforward, but the deployment of more complex tenses creates difficulties: 'She *has been* queen since 1953' (past perfect) or 'The Vikings *had discovered* America long before Columbus' (pluperfect). The most complex past tenses involve grammatical forms which express continuous or conditional relationships, and it is these which are most useful historically: 'The monarch *has been calling* parliament ever since . . .'; 'people *had been using* canals to transport goods before the coming of the railways'; and 'if Josiah Wedgwood *had been producing* coal and not pottery he might not have . . .'. In these cases it is not the thought but the means of the thought which causes the problems, yet this type of hesitant, 'time-layered' thinking is central to developing understandings of the past.

A further aspect of historians' language is the language of the organizing principles of history. The language of time and of change and historical description is an easily taken for granted element of historical knowledge. The language of time – year, century, millennium, era – is difficult for many pupils because of their own limited experience of time. Historians use the language and concept of time for more than to calibrate the sequencing of events. The idea of chronology and sequencing is meaningless in isolation; it becomes an element in the construction of knowledge about the past when it provides a framework for organizing ideas about historical change, historical causation and consequence. These organizing principles are the ways in which we help pupils to organize 'maps of the past': sets of ideas which give some meaningful shape to the past for learners. This language develops its own semi-specialist vocabulary. 'Chronology' is accompanied by ideas about 'periods', 'eras' and 'centuries' of rapid change (for example, the twentieth century) and those of relatively slow change or 'continuity' (for example, perhaps, the European Middle Ages). 'Causation' spawns a vocabulary of 'short term' and 'long term', or 'social', or 'economic', of 'primary' and 'secondary' significance, of 'sufficient' and 'necessary' causes. Denis Shemilt's research has done a great deal to clarify the sequence of development which characterizes adolescents' learning of such concepts, and, in consequence, the way adolescent learners make sense of the language of historical discourse.[5] Shemilt's models are not precise 'maps' of cognitive development, but they do offer a clear idea of the ways in which learning the conceptual underpinnings of historical language appears to progress (Table 3.1). Progressively more complex understandings of, for example, the concept of causation are associated with progressively more complex language to describe historical phenomena. The language of time has its own structures too: pupils need to learn to navigate not only through the mathematics of dates, but the grammar of eras, periods, and the conventions we use to describe the past. Historical description is drenched in linguistic convention.

Perhaps most complex of all, historical language itself is a vehicle for historical interpretation. Consider the events of 1640–60 in England. After the Restoration of Charles II, Clarendon, in the first significant narrative of the events described them as a 'Rebellion and Civils Wars in England', at a time when other

Table 3.1 Cognitive and language development in history: the example of understanding of causation

Stage 1
There is no logic of causation in history; things 'happen'; the 'story' 'unfolds'. Causation is unproblematic.

Stage 2
Causes are connected one to the other in sequence; an event 'had' to happen because of a mechanistic sequence of causes.

Stage 3
Causes are like scientific forces, acting in combination: 'unique' events were caused by a cluster of 'factors'. Some causes were clearly more important than others.

Stage 4
Causes are like a net: although individual causes ('knots in the net') may be significant, the relationship between the causes is as important. The relationships between these causes change over time.

Stage 5
There is a relationship between the nature of historical causes and the attribution of value given to them by historians; historians' models shape ideas about causation.

Stages 1–4 based on C. Sansom (1987) A developmental approach to the history syllabus in C. Portal (ed.) *The History Curriculum for Teachers*, p. 120. Lewes: Falmer. Stage 5 based on T. Lomas (1990) *Teaching and Assessing Historical Understanding*. London: Historical Association.

Royalist accounts referred to the 'horrid sin of Rebellion'. In the eighteenth and nineteenth centuries, historians referred to the 'Great Civil War' or, increasingly, the 'Great Rebellion' which became something of an academic commonplace in competition with the 'English Civil War'. At the end of the nineteenth century, emphasis on the religious as well as constitutional issues at stake introduced the label the 'Puritan Revolution'. In the twentieth century, broadening of historical focus and the development of a Marxist historiography of the events produced the label the 'English Revolution' which predated the French and Russian Revolutions. Most recently, academic research has examined events during the period outside the narrow confines of the English borders and labels emphasizing the 'British' context of the 'wars' or 'revolution' have gained currency. Now the difficult issue here is that the historical labels do not merely conceptualize descriptions, they also provide portmanteau interpretations of the events: are we studying a civil war or a revolution? An English or a British phenomenon? There is a language of historical interpretation and debate which shapes understanding in ways which may be unanticipated. The language we use to describe past events may validate some interpretations of them and, if only implicitly, rule out others. Indians, for example, do not describe the events of 1857 as an 'Indian Mutiny'. The difficulties we have with these words present real problems for language and its use in the classroom: shall we call the Indian Mutiny a 'mutiny'? Will we describe the events of 1640–60 as a civil war or a revolution?

All of this suggests that the linguistic difficulty of history is also what we can call an interpretive and epistemological difficulty: the way we describe the past also expresses a series of interpretations of it and the way we understand the past is inseparable from the way we know the past. These sorts of linguistic difficulty pose real problems in the classroom, but they are compounded because the typical encounter with them is not single but multiple. Concepts, ideas and historical language spill into each other at high speed. This is true of even relatively simple sentences. The statement 'In 1642 a Civil War broke out between King and Parliament' assumes grasp of a dating convention, familiarity with the concept of a Civil War (which was distinctive from, say the events in America between 1861 and 1865 or Russia between 1918 and 1921 or, recently, Bosnia-Herzegovina) and some understanding of the nature of kingship and role of Parliament in seventeenth century England. Most linguistic encounters in the history classroom are more complex yet, building up a web of overlapping concepts to sketch a general idea. The following passage from a school textbook makes the point about how authors assume prior *linguistic* and *conceptual* understandings in their reader:

> The growth of industry and the growth of the Empire are linked together by the need for foreign trade. Sea power made Britain a trading nation well before 1750. Raw materials [such as cotton from India] were brought to Britain, made into a finished product [such as cloth] and then sold abroad. The success of this trade encouraged the growth of industry. As industry grew more goods were produced and there was therefore a need for greater foreign trade.[6]

Does the language matter?

Do we need to consider the nature of historical language and the language of time? In one sense perhaps we do not: historical learning is part of pupils' wider education, an important aspect of which is the increasingly complex language development which flows from the encounter with new, unfamiliar and complex terminology. An awareness of historical language, of the complex meaning of revolution, or class, of the shifting meaning of kingship and the different nature of mills, or factories in the past may be an outcome of learning history.

In another sense, though, the nature of language is an important element in the teaching and learning of history. Underlying the analysis of language outlined in this chapter are two contrasting approaches to the function of language. In the first, the relationship between the past and the way we describe the past is relatively unproblematic: we use 'labels' to describe the past in ways which help us to understand it in terms of our own experience. Paying due attention to linguistic differences between past and present, we can understand the past through the language we deploy in the present; indeed, such language is one way of making the past comprehensible. This is not to argue that we should not use language as a labelling tool in history: in practice, these labels make historical discussion possible and they are one very important way in which we frame understandings of the past. It *is* important to construct simple schemes to unpack complex historical events and processes and to relate them to the way we describe events and processes in our own lives. But if we *only* use language in this way then we restrict both the historical understanding we can build up and the way we encourage children to think. We shall parody the past as a 'back-projection' of the present, assuming that the straightforward correspondence of language and the concepts of the past is a correspondence of ideas and analysis. We will make other people more like us than they may have been, and we will misconstrue the relationships they had with each other through what they said and wrote. We will be deaf to what people in the past meant if we restrict our use of language to labelling.

For this reason, the second approach to the function of language in history sketched here is more speculative. Language is a set of symbolic signs which allow us to communicate with others. Contemporary linguisticians[7] propose a distinction between the *signifier*, an image which acts as a vehicle and the *signified*, or the concept to which the signifier refers. Signifiers have no necessary meaning in themselves: they are arbitrary, and, as we have seen, changing sounds. The importance of signifiers comes from their being located in systems, or structures of signifiers which differ from each other. The word 'king' on its own means nothing. What brings meaning is both that the sounds on the page are different from the word 'lord' or 'peasant' and that it signifies a set of social and political relationships. This enables the signifier to be tied to the signified. The relationship is particularly complex when we are dealing with more abstract concepts: the word 'class' on its own means nothing but the structures of signifiers in which it appears will allow a biologist, a school manager, a historian or a left-wing politician to locate the 'meaning' of the word – the link between the signifier and the signified. The relationship between the components of our language and the signified to which language refers is in question. Language is a set of shifting interpretive signs; meanings shift from context to context and from learner to learner. The past is understood through and by words, words whose meaning is slippery or 'fuzzy'. This is a particular problem for teachers in schools, where the relationship between language and learning is critical.

The ideas we have about language powerfully affect the ideas we have about learning: if the relationship between the way we describe the past and the way the past 'was' is a direct one – if language provides a simple way of 'labelling' the past, then a number of implications flow about the sorts of classroom communication which need to be developed. Equally, if the relationship between the language in which we describe the past and the experiences of people in the past is viewed in more intepretive ways, then there are clear implications for teachers and learners. The different implications of these two ways of viewing language in the learning of history can be illustrated in Table 3.2, which is itself derived from one developed for science education by Clive Sutton.[7]

It is important to remember that the language being explored in this chapter is not *in itself* historical knowledge. The words and concepts are not in themselves reconstructions of past ways of life or societies or events. The language provides a set of organizing ideas around which historical reconstruction can be erected. What does follow are some implications for teacher talk and pupil talk, discussed in Chapter 7, of the way in which we use language to generate knowledge in the classroom. It is, however, important to enter a qualification here.

Teachers and talking

It is not a consequence of the argument being advanced here about the nature and function of language in the history classroom that teacher talk is less important than pupil talk, or that teachers should not 'teach' whole classes deploying exposition. Let us consider both propositions together.

Teachers of history have, through their education, reading and discussion, access to a wider framework of historical language and a wider frame of meaning than their pupils. The central function of the teacher is to teach. Teacher talk and the way teachers use talk is of critical importance in the way pupils learn. In the same way, teachers can speak more efficiently to the whole class than individual pupils or small groups for substantial elements of lessons without prejudicing the nature of learning. What *does* follow from this argument is the need to 'foreground' thinking about language in thinking about historical understanding, and

Table 3.2   Two approaches to language in history teaching

Language as a labelling system		Language as an interpretive system
Words correspond to objects and events in the past.	*What language says about the past and history*	Words shape thought and discourse about the past: we cannot experience the past other than through the words we choose to describe it.
Language is a way of communicating factual information about the past which the learner can then interpret.	*What language says about communication about the past*	Language is unpacked by different learners in different ways for different purposes. Learners need to explore, suggesting and thinking through words.
Clear language in clear exposition by the teacher is essential so that meanings are clear.	*What is the role of language in learning?*	Language priovides an opportunity to interpret and examine ideas.
Words have a fixed meaning which can be explained in definitions.	*What assumptions can we make about the meanings of words?*	Meanings are variable from learner to learners and from context to contexts. Definitions acquire meanings only in specific contexts.

for teachers to be conscious of the way they use interpretive language themselves and the way, in their lessons, opportunities for pupil talk relate to opportunities for teacher talk. Teachers need through their own talk to be aware of the interpetive nature of language, to understand that the language of history and the language of historical description are fuzzy and to use the opportunities they have for explaining and communicating to provide their pupils with opportunities to understand these aspects of language. Pupil talk is important, too, for the opportunities it gives pupils to explore language in the context of the history classroom: was this a 'civil war' or a 'revolution' is as important a question for pupils to discuss as 'what do you think were the causes of . . .'

Notes

1 On variation and change in meaning, the most useful and accessible text is R. Williams (1983) *Keywords*. London: Fontana, from which my material on 'revolution' is drawn. Also, A.C. Baugh and T. Cable (1978) *A History of the English Language*, 3rd edn, pp. 307–10. London: Routledge & Kegan Paul, suggest four aspects to change in meaning: extension/narrowing and degeneration/regeneration. D. Leith (1983) *A Social History of English*, pp. 70–2, 79. London: Routledge, distinguishes between six types of meaning, of which the most relevant here are his discussions of 'conceptual' meaning where a word is used for a broader idea (e.g. gentleman) and 'affective' meaning where a technical or specialist term becomes a term of approval/disapproval (e.g. 'fascist'). A cogent analysis of historian's work language is offered by P. Corfield (1991) *Language, History and Class*, pp. 1–23. Oxford: Blackwell.

2 On pupils' grasp of the language of the past, for the example quoted, see D. Barnes (1976) *From Communication to Curriculum*, p. 21. London: Penguin. Hilary Cooper offers an account of language and historical cognitive development in the early years of schooling in H. Cooper (1995) *History in the Early Years*. London: Routledge. Pupil understandings of historical language are explored in detail in M.D. Wilson (1985) *History for Pupils with Learning Difficulties*, pp. 54–79. London: Hodder and Stoughton, and in C. Morris (1992) Opening doors: learning history through talk in T. Booth, W. Swann, M. Masterton and P. Potts (eds) (1992) *Learning for All 1: Curricula for Diversity in Education*, pp. 20–33. London: Routledge. An extremely useful summary statement was ILEA (1983) Language and history in *History and Social Sciences at Secondary Level*, 2. London: ILEA, reprinted in H. Bourdillon (1994) *Teaching History*, pp. 122–5. London: Routledge, for the Open University.

3 On historians' use of 'everyday' language in specific contents, Tony Edwards' analysis of classroom language in history remains a lucid and relevant introduction. This paragraph draws extensively on: A.D. Edwards (1978) The 'language of history' and the communication of historical knowledge in A.K. Dickinson and P.J. Lee (eds) *History Teaching and Historical Understanding*, pp. 54–71. London: Heinemann.

Also D. Shemilt (1983) The devil's locomotive. *History and Theory*, 22: 1–18.

4 On the 'grammar' of history, I am grateful to Mark Quinn for guidance.

5 On pupils' grasp of the conceptual language of history, see D. Shemilt (1980) *History 13–16 Evaluation Study*. Edinburgh: Holmes McDougall. Also D. Shemilt (1984) Beauty and the Philosopher: empathy in history and the classroom in A.K. Dickinson, P.J. Lee and P. Rogers (eds) *Learning History*. London: Heinemann. Beverley Labbett argues that it is simply unhistorical to offer pupils ideas which give shape and meaning to the past without giving them the opportunity to explore and develop the meanings for themselves. See B.D.C. Labbett (1979) Towards a curriculum specification for history. *Journal of Curriculum Studies*, 11(2): 125–37.

6 Textbook language: the example is taken from R. Adams (1992) *Expansion Trade and Industry*, p. 36. Ormskirk: Causeway Press. History textbooks have been widely criticized, and over-reliance on textbooks certainly gives a false impression of the way in which history teachers present the past in the classroom. See P. Giles and G. Neal (1983) History teaching analysed in J. Fines (ed.) *Teaching History*, pp. 170–3. London: Macmillan. For a particular focus to the critique, see D. Gill (1987) History textbooks: education or propaganda. *Multicultural Teaching*, 7(2): 31–5.

7 The model of language outlined here derives from Saussurian linguistics and the redefinitions proposed by Derrida. I have relied on the accounts provided by V.P. Leitch (1983) *Deconstructive Criticism*. New York: Columbia University Press and C. Norris (1991) *Deconstruction: Theory and Practice*, 3rd edn, pp. 24–30. London and New York: Routledge. Saussure's central concern was to undo the link between 'word' and 'thing': meanings are bound up in linguistic systems of relationship and difference which underpin our thoughts and perceptions. Derrida takes this idea further: all words are associated with other words; all signs refer to other signs: all meaning is contingent on other meanings; no meanings are, therefore, simply present in words. I find useful Michael Shanks' discussion of language systems in relation to the past in his account of archaeological method; see M. Shanks (1991) *Experiencing the Past: on the character of archaeology*, pp. 30–1, 38–9. London: Routledge. My table is derived, with considerable modifications, from a similar one in C. Sutton (1992) *Words, Science and Learning*, p. 53. Milton Keynes: Open University Press. Generally, I have been heavily influenced by Sutton's thinking about the place of language in science teaching; his book is a model of lucidity and cogency and deserves to be read by history teachers as well as scientists.

Chapter 4

Historical forms:
narratives and stories

A third way to consider how which pupils and teachers make sense of the historical past is to think about the construction of accounts or versions of the historical past. The past has been represented through a variety of different types of accounts, among them, for example, chronicles, narrative stories, imaginative reconstructions and formal analytical essays. Stories have been an important way of rendering the past intelligible in most cultures, but their status in nineteenth and twentieth century historical thinking, and in classroom history, has become ambiguous: narrative is usually counterposed to 'analysis', 'story' to 'essay'. These oppositions are somewhat simplistic: narrative and analysis, story and essay may be complementary rather than competing ways of thinking about the past, serving different purposes. Jerome Bruner distinguishes between what he calls 'narrative' and 'paradigmatic' thinking:

> each providing distinctive ways of ordering experience, of constructing reality. . . . A good story and a well-formed argument are different natural kinds. Both can be used as means for convincing another. Yet what they convince of is fundamentally different: arguments convince of their truth, stories of their lifelikeness.[1]

Narrative thinking

The sense that 'the past' is distinct from 'history', that the experiences of people in the past are different from the meanings, shapes and understandings we have of their lives and experiences is a commonplace of modern historical thought. We marshal the past for different purposes on different occasions: the past is a source of moral saws ('Things never change'; 'You don't know how lucky you are'), of heroic celebration ('our glorious past') or triumph over adversity (the 'progress of education'; the 'rise of the Welfare State'); the past is a source of quirky eccentricities or of human fortitude in the face of suffering. The past provides us with the basis of an account of progress or of decline: we impose upon it the grand narratives of, for example, the 'Whig' or the 'Marxist' or the 'Weberian' interpretations of history, narratives with their beginnings, the turning points and their denouements.

Hayden White, a critic of the claims of modern historical work, suggests that all historical narratives follow four basic plots: comedy, tragedy, romance and satire, and notes that Ranke, one of the founders of modern historical studies, chose to 'write history emplotted as comedy'.[2] Narrative shapes of one form or another are ways of exploring these versions of the past, of rendering them accessible so that, in Bruner's terms they can then be considered and assessed paradigmatically. Indeed, narrative and paradigmatic thinking are complementary elements of historical discourse, or historical analysis: we give shapes to the past by 'storied' accounts, accounts which satisfy us by their logical consistency, their coherent relationship with the relics of the past and their 'lifelikeness', their 'feel' for what, as human beings, we think is likely to have been the case: we call upon not just the evidence, and not just our training in the methods and techniques of history, but our faculties as human beings to make the judgements we apply: 'it couldn't have been like that . . .'

Narrative shapes are built into the way we think about the past. This is true for both academic historians and pupils and teachers in classrooms, although the range, depth and purpose of the narrative shapes which are deployed in these different proceedings are sharply different. At their most basic, narrative shapes differentiate history from chronicle. Chronicles record events in unconnected and jumbled ways; histories sort events and organize them around ideas and labels in ways which give them meaning. Some of these narrative shapes are on the grand scale: they relate the rise, the consolidation and the fall of great empires over many centuries; there is a narrative of the rise and then the decline and fall of the Roman Empire; there is a narrative of the development of democracy in Britain. There is a narrative of the Industrial Revolution. We use narrative shapes on smaller scales too, where we use different words: we give a narrative shape to the French Revolution, to the First World War, to the sinking of the 'Lusitania'. We give a narrative shape to individuals' lives, where we call them 'biographies', and we select experiences from those lives to give shape, to give identity to the subject of the biography. In most of these cases, that which we are describing was not recognized by contemporaries; as Gordon Leff observes, 'what we recognise as the Roman Empire was a series of disconnected experiences for the generations who made it up. It is we who give them coherence'.[3] In all these cases we are using story to give a shape to experiences as a way of understanding them.

History and story

The relationship between history and story has always been a difficult one: the very definition of story (see Figure 4.1) shifts along the uneven border between fact and fiction, between truth and lies, between emotional and causal logic. Perhaps for this reason, historians and teachers have been sceptical about the place of story in the learning of history. Academic history has often been dismissive of 'mere' story: an unacademic, slightly immature and unreliable mode of analysis. History teachers, too, have more recently been dismissive of story: story, and narrative, have been associated with what David Sylvester calls the 'great tradition' of history teaching based around the 'active didacticism' of the history teacher relaying mainly British, mainly political history to essentially passive pupils.[4]

Yet in academic historiography, story has recently been reclaimed through the reconstruction of a 'storied' past organized around the lived experiences and representations of historical actors, of heretic peasant communities in medieval Languedoc, or sixteenth century Italian millers, eighteenth century plebeian cat-killers, and, most ambitiously, through the lived experiences of those 'citizens' who made the French Revolution: the mediation of the past through the storied experiences of those

Figure 4.1 History and story: some views on an imprecise relationship. Source: *Oxford English Dictionary*: emphases added.

He was in chirche a noble ecclesiaste,
Wel koude he rede a lesson or a storie
But alderbest he song an Offertorie.
G. Chaucer, *Canterbury Tales*, Prologue, 1.709–11 (1386)

Records of this Nation, without which no story of the Nation *can be written or proved.*
J. Chamberlayne, *Magnae Britanniae notitia; or The Present State of Great Britain*, i, iii, x, p. 220 (1708)

'Tis no Poet's Thought, no flight of Youth, but Solid Story and severest Truth.
Prior, *Ode in Imitation of Horace*, xii (1692)

A romance without a shadow of truth *may be exquisitely beautiful as a story.*
E.A. Freeman, *Historical Essays* (1866)

Story *is only a journalist's professional jargon for an* item of news. *The proper place for it is in a news bulletin.*
BBC, *The Task of Broadcasting News*, ii, 17 (1976)

You are always good children and never told stories.
John Wesley, *Journal*, 21 March (1770)

The unfortunate little victim was accordingly led below after receiving sundry thumps on the head from both his parents for having the wickedness to tell a story.
Charles Dickens, *BozSteam Excursions* (1834)

I also called at Mr Ducie's, who was indeede a rare collection of the best masters, and one of the largest stories of H. Holbein.
J. Evelyn, *Diary*, 8 May 1654

---

involved has proved to be a fruitful avenue for historical research and historical thinking. The starting point for much of this work came from outside history, from the cultural anthropology of Clifford Geertz, whose study of the significance of the cock fight in Bali introduced the concept of 'thick description'. Natalie Zemon Davies drew on Geertz's work for her study of Martin

Guerre, a sixteenth century wandering farmer who returned to his home in France to find that an imposter had taken over his farm and his wife. Peter Burke points out that the book can be read as a story because this is the way in which Natalie Zemon Davies chose to organize her account, which nonetheless casts light on the values and assumptions of early modern peasant society. Davies writes:[5]

> I choose to advance my arguments as much by the
> ordering of narrative, choice of detail, literary voice and
> metaphor as by topical analysis.

In this reshaped narrative tradition, storied forms are used to address wider, more complex ideas, and to stimulate *ways of thinking* about the past and about the ways in which the past was experienced. It becomes possible through the narrative to address more abstract ideas about the assumptions and beliefs of past societies, about the ways they worked or failed to work, and about how people represented their relationships with each other. This development in academic historiography appears closely related to the way in which pupils in school think as they try to make sense of a bewildering and confusing past. For them, too, story has a powerful heuristic, analytical function in history.

> Underlying pupils' thinking . . . seems to be the idea of a
> past which happens in stories. Stories are given in the
> unfolding of events.[6]

The delusions and potentials of story

One of the difficulties of narrative modes in the history classroom has always been the way in which they appear to locate the power to shape meaning in the hands of the teacher. In narrative, the teacher chooses the characters to include, the language in which to describe them and imputes words to them. She chooses a starting point – the place at which this narrative will begin – and brings the story to an end. For the skilled storyteller, these powers bring with them the power to shape reactions and to direct emotions towards one account rather than another, so that, as Grant Bage points out:[7]

when the teacher 'takes for granted' the moral basis or outcome of the story of an episode in history, the children learning from it are denied the opportunity to critically and democratically decide their own version or interpretation of what 'this story means or shows'. . . . They are victims, passive targets of the moralising history story rather than its critical audience.

Storytellers can oversimplify; they sketch characters as carica-tures and complex situations as archetypes of good and evil; they impose coherence where there is none; they impose structure, finding for their stories a beginning, a middle and an end which is *their* beginning, middle and end where other interpretations are possible; they impose on their stories a logic of causation and of sequence which draws their readers and their listeners from the point they have identified as their beginning securely to the point which they identify as the end. When their story ends, the characters and events they have selected and sketched end with them. The endings of stories close down emotion and thought. Stories confuse the boundary between fact and fiction: indeed, we typically value storytellers for the fictive elements they impose on story, the ways in which they make the story 'theirs'. Stories promote acceptance; they close down possibilities and can in consequence exclude questioning. All this is true, and is at odds with the provisional, questioning history which teachers strive for.

Yet storytellers have other powers too: they can entrance the imagination, conjure a picture of the past which is vivid and immediate, give 'life' to the characters they describe, create excitement and interest. Storytellers make us laugh, and make us cry, they make us want to pursue the tale, they conjure aural and mental images which shape the way we think about the past: they stimulate our interest and our curiosity. The fictional elements of stories raise questions, demand that we enquire further, extend our conceptions of the interpretations which the evidence permits. Used in this way, stories arouse, not dampen curiosity, they draw in the listener to the texture of the tale, they provoke and frustrate and hence encourage further investigation. Stories told well remind us that the outcomes of past events were never given or inevitable but contingent on human agency and un-expected interventions. If many of the themes of history are abstract, story is human-scale; thinking through stories remains one important way of developing meanings, or advancing interpretations. The historical limitations of many stories are more readily apparent than their personal value, but stories attempt to make sense of alien contexts experiences.

The teller of history stories is bounded by obligations to the past she describes; to suggest that story has an important role in the representation of the past is not to say that it may be immediately substituted for the structured past of logic and causation, of argument and development but to remind ourselves that we approach the past through human experience. In fact, there is a degree of consensus about what the obligations of the storyteller are. There is an obligation of accuracy to what can be derived from historical evidence.[8] The evidence does not predetermine the shape of the story, but it clearly sets boundaries around the range of possible stories which can be told. We cannot represent the Battle of Waterloo as a victory for the French, or the outcome of the Throckmorton Plot as the overthrow of Elizabeth I; the skill of the storyteller may reside in her ability to present the outcomes as unforeseeable or unanticipated: the shock of the unexpected, the twist which we had not anticipated, but she will owe an obligation of accuracy to that element of the historical record which is agreed and which could otherwise falsify her account. The second is an obligation of authenticity to period and character, and by implication credibility to historical dialogue. Julius Caesar cannot arrive by plane, nor workhouse inmates become bored by television. Finally, and less obviously, the storyteller must be aware that her story is not the only, or the definitive version of the tale: there are 39 extant versions of the tale of Red Riding Hood, and there are different possible, plausible accounts of any historical story: the teller has an obligation of openness to other versions of the story.

Beyond this, there is no storytelling without listener, no written narrative without a reader. In preliterate societies, oral tradition was one of the most important ways in which public memories were preserved and communicated:[9] stories were created in the telling. If there are obligations on the storyteller, on the teacher as storyteller, there are obligations on the listener too. No story is simply 'received', no story is simply 'heard': we remake the story, when we recount it, when we begin to think about the sequence, the characters, the eventuation. Listeners have an active role in the story; indeed, their reactions during the telling of the story – the expressions of interest, or boredom, of apathy or of concern – shape the story. The pauses, the hesitations, the twists and the turns have to be interpreted by the listener: the story is hers as much as it is the teller's. So narrative is far from supposing the compliance of a passive listener. Storying is one of the ways we recount, and hence reshape, the interpretation we place upon the past. In classrooms, the obligations on the storytellers impose obligations on the listeners, to go further than the story, to pose questions about it, to examine its consistency with the evidential remains, to offer further interpretations, to examine its authenticity and its representations of character, time and place. The telling of stories calls forth further stories. Story, I am arguing, is a means to an end; to the making of historical understanding. It is not an end in itself: the end is the generation of understandings about the past, and this turns on the thinking of the learner.

In an important sense, story is about humanizing the past, about relating its complexity and the broader themes of historical scholarship to a form where we can work on them and attach usable meanings to them. Narratives are an integrative component in historical thinking. 'Storied thinking' is a central tool in the teaching and learning of history, provided that both listener and teller, pupil and teacher play out their obligations to the logic of the narrative. If story is central to the way pupils think about the past, then stories need to be explored in classrooms. This means telling stories, but also asking pupils to recount stories; it means subjecting stories to critical examination, making sense of what I have called their lifelikeness as well as their logic. It involves a constructively sceptical doubt about the nature of the stories we tell. It means relating stories to those 'organizing principles' – the ideas of causation, continuity, change – of complex historical discourse

Notes

1 On storied thinking, see J. Bruner (1986) *Actual Minds, Possible Worlds*, p. 11. Harvard: Harvard University Press. My own thinking about story has been considerably developed through my acquaintance with the work of Grant Bage. See Grant Bage (1995) 'Chaining the Beast: an

examination of how the pedagogic use of spoken stories may make historical narrative richer and more susceptible to analysis by children. An autobiographical research study by an advisory teacher'. Unpublished PhD thesis, University of East Anglia; see especially Chapters 2–5, pp. 36–153. Bage offers both a rationale for the centrality of story in thinking and, which is perhaps even more powerful, a superb analysis of the classroom use of the story of King Edmund which demonstrates storied history in the service of historical understanding at its very best.

2 On storied histories, the critical account is set out in Hayden White (1973) *Metahistory*, pp. 176–7. Baltimore: Johns Hopkins Press, quoted in Peter Burke (1991b) The history of events in Peter Burke (ed.) *New Perspectives on Historical Writing*, p. 239. Oxford: Polity Press. White's ideas are examined for their relationship to recent British social historiography in A. Wilson (1993) A critical portrait of social history in A. Wilson (ed.) *Rethinking Social History: English society 1570–1920 and its interpretation*, pp. 24–5. Manchester: Manchester University Press.

3 On shaping the past through narratives, see G. Leff (1969) *History and Social Theory*. p. 105. London: Merlin Press. David Lowenthal (1985) *The Past is a Foreign Country*, pp. 221–2. Cambridge: Cambridge University Press, quotes Richard Cobb's view that a sequence of identifiable monarchs in England structures a 'time scale . . . understandable to any . . . child', and Penelope Lively (p. 223) describes the same sequence of 'nice, linear, uninterrupted memory'. Lowenthal comments that 'narrative's linear nature does constrain historical understanding. Yet . . . historical intelligibility requires not merely past events occurring at particular times but a coherent story in which . . . temporal sequence is often subordinated to explanation and interpretation. Just as we think back and cast ahead in recapitulating . . . [so effective] narratives back-track to clarify causal connections'.

4 On the 'great tradition', see D. Sylvester (1994) Change and continuity in history teaching, 1900–1993, in H. Bourdillon (ed.) *Teaching History*, pp. 9–25. London: Routledge, for the Open University.

5 On narrative approaches in recent historical work, see the notion of 'thick description' set out in the essay on the Balinese cock fight by Clifford Geertz (1972) *The Interpretation of Cultures*. London: Hutchinson. Narrative accounts of historical ideas are deployed in a variety of ways in Simon Schama (1989) *Citizens: a chronicle of the French Revolution*. New York: Knopf, Robert Darnton (1984) *The Great Cat Massacre and Other Episodes in French Cultural History*. New York: Basic Books, and Carlo Ginzburg (1980) *The Cheese and the Worms: the cosmos of a sixteenth-century miller*. Baltimore: Johns Hopkins Press. I draw on Natalie Zemon Davies here and in the next chapter: N.Z. Davies (1973) *The Return of Martin Guerre*. Cambridge: Massachusetts; the quotation is from N.Z. Davies (1988) On the lame. *American Historical Review*,

93:575. See also Lawrence Stone (1979) The revival of narrative: reflections on a new old history. *Past and Present*, 85: 1–20. For the use of a storied biography, see Beverley Labbett (1990) Muriel Wakefield, *Cambridge Journal of Education*, 20(3): 207–32. See also Raphael Samuel (1990a) Grand narratives. *History Workshop Journal*, 29: 120–32, especially p. 127: 'History's narratives, however compelling, are always provisional.'

6 On pupils' sense of 'story', the quotation is from Peter Lee (1991) Historical knowledge and the national curriculum in R. Aldrich (ed.) *History in the National Curriculum*, p. 54. London: Kogan Page. Hilary Cooper (1995) *History in the Early Years*, pp. 50–6. London: Routledge, makes the point that stories are important in the cognitive development of young children: 'stories affect children's intellectual growth for they do not listen passively; they are called upon to create new worlds through powers of imagination. . . . Stories extend first hand experiences of the world . . . so extending perceptions of the world' (p. 50). Writing about adults' views of the past, Lowenthal, op. cit., p. 223, quotes James Henretta's argument that narrative 'approximates to the reality of everyday life; most readers view the past in the same manner as they comprehend their own existence . . . in terms of a series of overlapping and interwoven life stories'.

7 On the dangers of story, see Bage, 'Chaining the Beast', p. 49. Bage quotes Valerie Chancellor's verdict: 'Of all subjects history is perhaps the most obviously a vehicle for the opinions of the teacher and of the section of society he represents. It gives scope for the expression of a wide variety of political, mortal and religious ideas and since these are embedded in a traditional and often emotive story they are aguably more open to acceptance and less liable to detection by the pupil.' See V. Chancellor (1970) *History for their Masters: history in the school textbook, 1800–1914*, p. 8. London: Penguin.

8 On the effective use of story in the classroom, this paragraph owes a great deal to V. Little and T. John (1990) *Historical Fiction in the Classroom*. London: Historical Association, Teaching of History Series 59. More generally, see Grant Bage, op. cit. The information about Red Riding Hood derives from Robert Darnton, op. cit., p. 18.

9 On storytelling in preliterate societies, see Jan Vansina (1978) *Oral Tradition as History*. Oxford: Oxford University Press. Vansina shows both the centrality of oral traditions and narratives of the past in preliterate societies and the ways in which transformations of tradition operate in ways which allow stories to reflect shifting concerns. Gwyn Prins explores oral traditions more generally, distinguishing between representations of 'unstructured time' (myths of genesis), 'traditional time' (sequenced but not serial) and our own conception of 'serial' time; see Gwyn Prins (1991) Oral history in P. Burke (ed.) op. cit., pp. 123–6.

Chapter 5

Historical forms: facts, fictions and imagination

One of Jane Austen's characters expressed surprise at the dullness of history 'when so much of it must be invention', and at this point, we must consider an important aspect of the nature of historical narrative and understanding: the use of the imagination in the reconstruction of the historical past. What, for teachers and pupils, is the place of the imagination in the reconstruction of the past?

Historical imagination in the classroom

History education up to the 1960s was generally characterized by approaches to history which encouraged the learning of 'hard', 'empirical' information about the past and hence was sceptical about the place of the imagination in history. The Schools Council History Project (1972–78) posed a significant challenge to the tradition, insisting that whilst 'imagination must be disciplined by the evidence available', the pupil, like the historian:[1]

> has to be able to enter into the mind and feeling of all the people involved in an event and appreciate their differing attitudes without necessarily approving of their motives if he is to understand why . . . they acted as they did . . . history demands an exercise in imagination or an ability to enter into the past sympathetically.

The elevation of the role of imagination in this way legitimated classroom practices which asked pupils to write imaginative diaries, to consider how they might react in the situation of Martin Luther, to consider the ideas and assumptions of a factory worker of the 1830s or the motivation of Oliver Cromwell, or Elizabeth I. Put in this way, the exercise of the imagination is, like the construction of different types of narrative, a form of *historical explanation* which depends on combining a disciplined under-standing of historical context, narrative skills and the use of historical imagination. But increasingly, the use of 'empathy' – as a shorthand for the exercise of the imagination in constructing historical accounts – caused difficulties for some educators who found it a clumsy and unconvincing historical tool which posed curriculum and assessment problems.

The print in Figure 5.1 purports to show a vagrant being whipped through the streets of an Elizabethan town. To what classroom uses can we put this evidence? Can the history teacher, over and beyond using this as an *illustration* of the sort of treatment vagrants might receive under the Poor Laws in the later sixteenth century, ask pupils to consider what it felt like to be the beggar, or to consider the attitudes to poverty of those observing, or to consider the *mentalité* of the man wielding the whip? These questions are useful because they allow us to define clearly the three elements to the charge against the use of the historical imagination, all of which can be applied to the sorts of tasks which might engage pupils in thinking about the plight of our Elizabethan vagrant.

The first element concerns historical imagination being an imprecise tool which makes external verification and judgement of the accounts it produces almost impossible. Even if it were possible to reconstruct the ideas and assumptions of people in the past, against what criteria would we judge one pupil's recon-struction of the vagrant's compared to another pupil's work? What is 'good' and what is 'bad'? More crudely, how do we differentiate between historical 'facts' and imaginative 'fictions'? This is the verification charge against the use of the imagina-tion.

The second element concerns the tasks described resting on a tempting but simple fallacy. The 'vagrant' in the print never existed; at best, he is an archetype; such vagrants left no 'evidence' and it is futile to suppose that we can reconstruct their world-view. The representation was itself constructed according to certain rules and for a particular purpose. The past is *always*

Figure 5.1 Tudor print showing a beggar being whipped. Reproduced by permission of the Syndics of Cambridge University Library.

refracted through some observer's lens or other, so that it is wrong to believe that that the 'evidence' allows us access to a different world-view. For this reason, the use of historical evidence for this sort of imaginative exercise inevitably distorts the past. The exercise of the imagination has little to do with the past and more to do with the evocation of 'sympathy' for particular historical individuals and groups. By extension, such activities mean that we can manipulate the past: this becomes 'history for political purposes' and means that learners' understandings are themselves open to manipulation. This is the evidential charge against the use of the imagination.

The third element denies that the ideas and beliefs of people in the past can *in principle* be reconstructed: the gap between our own mindset and that of people in the past is so great, and the evidential materials so weak that no intellectually valid reconstruction can be attempted. It is, indeed, logically impossible to 'enter other minds'; for pupils, the exercise of empathy in effect involves making all historical actors like us: rational, calculating, feeling individuals. This is the historicist charge against the use of the imagination.[2]

These are powerful arguments and their importance cannot be underestimated. However I argue that they can be countered if we think again about the relationship between history and fictional accounts of the past. We need to consider carefully the way in which we ask pupils to exercise imagination in constructing versions of the past by examining the intellectual procedures involved in imaginative understandings of the past.

The boundaries between fact and fiction

History teachers, like historians, used to believe that they dealt in facts and that their work reflected the reality of the past. This belief has been shattered by recent assaults from philosophy and linguistics: some philosophers, indeed, now claim that historians, like novelists, are concerned with fiction, producing accounts according to literary rules and styles. The main critic has been Hayden White who has accused historians of operating within dated, nineteenth century, conventions of what constitutes 'realism', and who believes that it is necessary:

> to force historians to abandon the attempt to portray 'one particular portion of life *right side up* and in *true* perspective' . . . and to recognise that there is no such thing as a *single* correct view. . . . This would allow us to entertain seriously those creative distortions offered by minds capable of looking at the past with the same seriousness as ourselves but with different orientations. Then we should not longer naïvely expect that statements about a given epoch or complex of events in the past 'correspond' to some pre-existent body of 'raw facts'. For we should recognise that *what constitutes the facts themselves* is the problem that the historian . . . has tried to solve in the choice of the metaphor by which he orders his world, past, present and future.

For White:

> How else can any past which by definition comprises events, processes, structures and so forth which are no

longer perceivable, to be represented . . . except in an
imaginary way?[3]

The border between 'facts' and 'fictions' has become indistinct.
Novelists have drawn on 'historical reality' for their work. For
example, Thomas Keneally's Booker prize-winning novel *Schindler's Ark* (1983) claims to use the 'devices of a novel to tell a true
story' of a German diplomat's attempts to save Jews from death
camps. Norman Mailer's *The Armies of the Night* (1968) about a
protest march is subtitled 'History as a Novel/The novel as
History'. Adam Thorpe's novel about the English countryside
Ulverton (1985) uses pastiche and historical forms to explore
different ideas about the nature of the past and of historical
change. Other novelists incorporate documents, or press-
cuttings into the text of their work; yet others undermine
traditional narrative notions of realism by including flashbacks,
untrustworthy narrators, alternative conclusions. On the other
hand, historians have experimented with fictional forms, most
notably Simon Schama's imaginative account of episodes for
which there is no extant evidence in his *Dead Certainties:
Unwarranted Speculations* (1983).

In other parts of this border territory, apparent fiction and
apparent history meet head on. In 1941, Janet Lewis published a
novella based on a sixteenth century French legal case of marital
desertion and personation, which she called *The Wife of Martin
Guerre*. Lewis notes that she had not read the key legal papers on
the case first published in 1572, but only a nineteenth century
popularized and translated account.

In 1982, the American cultural historian Natalie Zemon Davies
collaborated with the film-maker Daniel Vigne to make the film *Le
Retour de Martin Guerre*. Later, with some misgivings about the
film, Davies produced her 'academic' account *The Return of Martin
Guerre* drawing both on the sixteenth century archives and her
reading of twentieth century anthropology and literary criticism.
Davies notes that 'what I offer here is in part my invention, but
held tightly in check by the voices of the past'; one of her critics
suggests that Davies's account is as 'inventive' and 'fictional' as
Lewis's.

If this is border territory between 'facts' and 'fictions', other
accounts suggest that the no-man's land is wide indeed. Natalie
Zemon Davies' most recent work examines 'fiction in the

archives', a study of the place of narrative techniques and rhetorical forms in sources such as the depositions of witnesses, the examinations of suspects and pleas for pardons in sixteenth century French courts. She begins by observing that she was once taught 'to peel away the fictive elements in our documents so that we could get at the hard facts', but then argues that the act of storytelling is itself a worthwhile historical theme: the fictions become history.[4] It has long been recognized that fictions themselves can contribute distinctive elements to the understanding of the past:[5]

> imaginative truth . . . transcends what the historian can give you: . . . history cannot come so near to human hearts and human passions as a good novel can. . . . To make a bygone age live again history must not be merely eked out by fiction; . . . it must be turned into a good novel.

The historical imagination

If the boundaries between history and fiction are no longer clear or distinct, if, indeed the argument is that understanding the past is itself a *creative* act which can be rendered differently by historians, novelists and poets, then the place of the imagination in the construction of historical accounts becomes central. Historical understanding depends as much on how we think about the past, how we formulate questions to ask about the past and how we go about organizing answers to the questions as on the information we collect by reading, looking and sifting information. Accounts of the place of the imagination in contemporary historical practice generally derive from the work of R.G. Collingwood.[6] In *An Autobiography*, Collingwood outlined an idealist philosophy of history based on the imaginative reconstruction of past patterns of thought and perceptions. For Collingwood, historical investigation depended on using evidence which had itself been created for a purpose; consequently, the 'reconstruction' of the past depended on understanding what purposes were in the mind of the historical actors who created the evidence. Collingwood went on to set in opposition two forms of logical argument in history and philosophy: what he called *propositional logic* and what he called his own *'question and answer' logic*. In modern historical thinking, the dichotomy translates into two types of historical reconstruction: history 'from the outside' and 'history from the inside'. The former is concerned with the analysis of, for example, demographic and social structures, or with political and constitutional events and their consequences. The latter is concerned with cultural social and intellectual history, with the ways in which people in the past believed and thought. *Because* the evidential base for historical reconstructions is characterized by *lacunae* and deliberate omission, 'history from the inside' involves the application of the imagination: imagination in asking questions, imagination in answering them. One of the most eminent of twentieth century historians argued that it was:

> more important that the initial perception should be sharp and vivid than that it should be true. Truth comes from error more easily than from confusion. It is only by having a vivid perception that an energetic search can begin.[7]

A year or two after the outbreak of war [in 1914] I was living in London and working with a section of the Admiralty Intelligence Division in the rooms of the Royal Geographical Society. Every day I walked across Kensington Gardens and past the Albert Memorial. The Albert Memorial began by degrees to obsess me. . . . Everything about it was visibly mis-shapen, corrupt, crawling, verminous; for a time I could not bear to look at it and passed with averted eyes; recovering from this weakness, I forced myself to look and to face day by day the questions: a thing so obviously, so incontrovertibly, so indefensibly bad, why had Scott done it? To say that Scott was a bad architect was to burke the problem with a tautology; to say that there was no accounting for tastes was to evade it by *suggestio falsi*. . . . What relation was there, I began to ask myself between what he had done and what he had tried to do? . . . I began by observing that you cannot find out what a man means by simply studying his spoken or written statements, even though he has spoken or written with perfect command of language and perfectly truthful intention. In order to find out his meaning you must also know what the question was to which the thing he has had or written was meant as an answer.

From: R.G. Collingwood (1939) *An Autobiography*, pp. 29–30. Oxford: Oxford University Press.

Historical imagination and the use of systematic doubt

Critics of the use of the imagination in history and particularly in school history worry that the use of the imagination leads to flights of wild fantasy in which the premium is on creativity rather than on the disciplines of historical context. In their model of understanding the past, learning history is fairly mechanical. Sources are found, questioned, assembled and used to reconstruct an explanation of the past. On this model, the scope of the historical imagination is limited to plausibly filling gaps in the record so that a 'true' or most 'plausible' account can be rendered.

Yet most historical investigation appears to work quite differently. Questions about the past inevitably presuppose an act of creative imagination. And the actions of historical individuals, their relationships with each other and the assumptions or systems of belief which gave rise to their actions are never completely captured in the evidence which is left behind. Indeed, it may well be difficult to separate the process of research and the process of reconstruction. Far from simply involving the dogged accumulation of historical material, research appears to depend on the deployment of other skills, as Jan Vansina explores:

Josephine Tey's novel, *The Daughter of Time* features a police sergeant who . . . exemplified historical practice – he guesses, ponders, backtracks, and finds sources almost by intuition. If he had made a few more mistakes he would have been a recognisable historian at work. . . . In the real world, historians start out with a hunch, an idea, which leads them to an interest in documents or in oral traditions. Then the data suggest what Popper calls a historical

interpretation – 'untestable points of view'. The practitioner
feels that the interpretation is not enough. It should be
doubted and controlled by reference to more data until the
point is reached at which no more control is possible. Then
the historian feels satisfied with the result, even though it
still remains an interpretation.

These 'hunches', this 'intuition', are central to the way we look
for and make sense of historical evidence in the record office and
the classroom. The relationships between the historian and his,
or her material, are complex ones. For Vansina, working at the
edges of the historical record in Africa, the sharpest-edged tool of
the historian was human intuition allied to what he called the
power of systematic doubt. Writing from a liberal historical tradition,
Hexter drew historians' attention to what he called the historian's
second record: the ways in which in order to confer 'meaning'
on the evidential remains of the past, historians draw, often
subconsciously, on their own assumptions, experiences and
imaginative faculties. In the construction of historical understanding, the historian is not a cipher, but an active participant in
the dialogue between the present and the past. In the classroom,
in understanding the past, the pupil is not an empty vessel, but
an active agent: current concerns, the perspectives of the present
are an integral part of the process of understanding history. What
pupils bring into school shapes the ways in which they can work
on the materials we ask them to examine and the questions they
pose of these materials.[8]

Controlling the historical imagination

Dissolving the boundaries between fact and fiction, placing at the
centre of the process of historical understanding the deployment
of the 'second record' and the 'power of systematic doubt',
accepting that 'hunches' are central to understanding the past
provides us with a quite different account of the historical process
from that sketched by critics of the deployment of imagination.
The exercise of the imagination in some form turns out to be
central to the development of any sort of investigation or
understanding of the past. It is, in many ways, an uncomfortable
picture. Once we question the 'factual' nature of history, do we

have any stable basis for preferring one interpretation to another, for 'verifying' accounts against an 'evidential' base? How do we distinguish between thoughtful arguments and sheer fantasy? Thirty years ago, E.H. Carr spoke of a 'dialogue' between the historian and the evidence, and more recent accounts of the relationship have suggested the active nature of this dialogue, so that each attempt to describe historical events, whether in the record office, the seminar room or the classroom relies on the deployment of imagination and assumptions about the past: we make assumptions about how people react to events, to other people and to their own experiences; our assumptions are modified by the encounter with the physical remains of the past, and so generate a set of hypotheses about the past which are then further modified by further acquaintance with historical evidence, but also by our reflections, by discussion and so on. The 'dialogue' is between ourselves and our often tacit assumptions and the past which:[9]

> has its own voices that must be respected, especially when they resist or qualify the interpretations we would like to place on them.

This receptiveness to the *experiences* and *assumptions* of historical actors is critical and provides an initial control on the liberation of imagination in the construction of historical understanding, but if the relationship between 'facts' and 'fictions' in understanding the past is an insecure one, how can we distinguish between different imaginative interpretations? How can we assess the working of the historical imagination?

The most helpful recent discussion of this general question is provided by the philosopher Mark Bevir. Like most recent philosophers, Bevir rejects the empiricists' idea of a 'given' past which can be understood if we accumulate enough information. His reason for doing so is that our perceptions of the past always depend on theories and categories which come from our own experience. For this reason, ideas about the past cannot be 'verified' or 'falsified'. However, Bevir argues that sets of ideas about the past *can* be compared and criticized if we use what he calls a logic of comparison. Historians generate 'webs of interpretation' and understandings arise from 'criticising and comparing webs of interpretations in terms of . . . evidence which nearly everyone in a given community would accept as true'.[10] Bevir's

Figure 5.2   Mark Bevir's criteria for evaluating historical explanations.

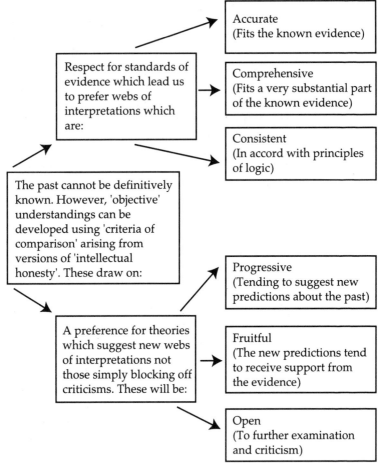

Respect for standards of evidence which lead us to prefer webs of interpretations which are:

Accurate
(Fits the known evidence)

Comprehensive
(Fits a very substantial part of the known evidence)

Consistent
(In accord with principles of logic)

The past cannot be definitively known. However, 'objective' understandings can be developed using 'criteria of comparison' arising from versions of 'intellectual honesty'. These draw on:

A preference for theories which suggest new webs of interpretations not those simply blocking off criticisms. These will be:

Progressive
(Tending to suggest new predictions about the past)

Fruitful
(The new predictions tend to receive support from the evidence)

Open
(To further examination and criticism)

'criteria of comparison' (see Figure 5.2) provide what he calls 'rules of thumb' for comparing historical interpretations and they are both useful and usable. Bevir's argument is helpful to us in appraising historical ideas of any sort. Instead of the confusing question 'is this true?' or 'is this right?' we can pose questions derived from Bevir's rational processes: 'Does this account – compared to others – meet our criteria for judging ideas?'

Historical understanding and moral judgement

There are, of course, problems which arise precisely because of the extent to which understanding the past depends on the exercise of the creative imagination. One of the most difficult elements of school history remains its relationship to the social and moral purposes of education. The study of the Slave Trade, or the Holocaust, is not simply an exercise in academic reconstruction but in schools remains in many ways a profoundly *moral* exercise: we are concerned as much with concepts of humanity and inhumanity as with those of evidence and change. One of the justifications for school history, and for the inclusion of the eighteenth century Slave Trade or the extermination camps of Nazi Germany, remains its capacity to provide a framework within which we can ask pupils to confront human action and moral judgement.

A class of 15-year olds examined the testimony of Holocaust survivors. The lesson was about the Holocaust, linking the events at Treblinka, Belsen and Auschwitz to the context of Nazi ideology, but Robert, before we could ask, or answer any of the historical questions, bravely encapsulated what he and many of his classmates were thinking: 'I find this very difficult. I can't think about this as history. What's here is horrible; I can't cope with it.' Looking at pictorial representations of live slave ships, a 14-year old girl's pained question, 'But how could they *do* that?' is not simply a historical question about attitudes in the eighteenth century, but a moral and human question too; in schools, at least, there are obligations to address both sets of questions. We *teach* and *learn* history in schools in a moral and social context; there *are* differences between the obligations of teachers and the obligations of professional historians. Part of the responsibility of the history teacher is to support the development of moral judgement, and a key component of such development has to be the exercise of the imagination, the understanding that historical events had human consequences and were experienced by people different from ourselves, but nonetheless by people. In this sense, the historical imagination is not, as some have presented it, an escapist device, but a hard-edged and uncomfortable tool. This is not to suggest that, in some Victorian manner, we should see history as a 'source of moral examples'. On the other hand:

Only we, who are now living can give a 'meaning' to the past. But that past has always been among other things, the result of an argument about values. In recovering that process, in showing how causation actually eventuated, we must, insofar as the discipline can enforce, hold our own values in abeyance. But once this history has been recovered we are at liberty to offer our judgement upon it. Such judgement must itself be under historical controls. . . . Our vote will change nothing. And yet, in another sense, it may change everything. For we are saying that these values and not . . . other values, are the ones which make this history meaningful *to us*, and that these are the values which we intend to enlarge and sustain in our own present.[11]

It is to enhance the humanism of history teaching that we need a less restrictive attitude to imagination. We have to encourage the development of imaginative reconstructions of the past *as well as* explanatory and narrative understandings. For this reason, we should be more tolerant of confusions and more tolerant of mis-understandings which we encounter while pupils attempt to make sense of the 'otherness' of past people and societies. Caution and scepticism are important, but they are not enough. In the classroom, we need to engage emotions as well as intellects.

Can the past be understood on any terms without the exercise of the imagination?
How is one to address oneself without a persistent feeling of fatuity, even of indecency to the theme of ultimate inhumanity?
George Steiner (1971) *In Bluebeard's Castle*, p. 31.
London: Faber & Faber.

Elizabeth I began to be a little more incensed against the Puritans. . . . And indeed within a few days after, John Stubbs of Lincoln's Inn, a fervent, hot-headed Professor of religion, . . . the author of this book, William Page who dispersed the copies and Singleton the printer were apprehended. Against whom sentence was given that

their right hands should be cut off. . . . Hereupon Stubbs
and Page had their right hands cut off with a cleaver driven
through the wrist by the force of a mallet, upon a scaffold
in the market place at Westminster. The printer was
pardoned. I remember, being there present, that when
Stubbs after his right hand was cut off put off his hand
with his left and said with a loud voice, 'God Save the
Queen!'

Camden, W. (1623) *History of the Princess Elizabeth*.

'Because the small children at their mothers' breasts were a
great nuisance during the shaving, the children were taken
from their mothers as soon as they got off the train. The
children were taken in an enormous ditch, they were shot
and thrown into the fire. No-one bothered to see if they
were really dead. Sometimes one could hear infants
wailing in the fire. If mothers managed to keep their babies
with them a guard took the baby by its legs and smashed it
against the wall until only a bloody mess remained in his
hands. The mother then had to take this mess with her to
the 'bath'.

An eye-witness account of the Treblinka death camp,
quoted in C. Shephard et al. (1993) *Peace and War*,
London: John Murray.

Notes

1 On what empathy is, see Schools Council (1976) *A New Look at History*, p. 18. Edinburgh: Holmes McDougall. For a refinement of the definition, see HMI (1985) *History in the Primary and Secondary Years*, p. 3. London: HMSO: 'the ability to enter into some informed appreciation of the predicaments of people in the past: it depends on the ability to interpret evidence, be aware of anachronism, and to forget what we know about the outcome of past evidence'. The definition is contested. John Slater correctly points out that empathy 'is *not* [original emphasis] the same as wholly identifying with people in the past, which would be impossible' (though some critics see it as precisely this) nor is it 'sympathising with them which could be morally as well as historically dubious' and Christopher Portal notes that one of the difficulties in the debate over empathy is that it is 'still

at best a shorthand term for a cluster of related notions'. See John Slater (1989) *The Politics of History Teaching: a humanity dehumanised?* p. 7. Special Professorial Lecture, London: Institute of Education and C. Portal (1987) Empathy as an objective for history teaching in C. Portal (ed.) *The History Curriculum for Teachers*, pp. 62–3. Lewes: Falmer. Some recent work on 'empathy' fails to adopt a clear definition of empathy, or deploys a loose and theoretically indefensible definition: see A. Farmer and P. Knight (1994) *Active History in Key Stages 3 and 4*, pp. 11–12. London: David Fulton, for an example of the first and R. Brooks, M. Aris and I. Perry (1994) *The Effective Teaching of History*, p. 112. Harlow: Longman, for an example of the second.

2 On the critique of empathy, see Keith Jenkins (1991) *Rethinking History*, pp. 44–6. London: Routledge. Jenkins argues that empathy is procedurally impossible and that it has become popular for its relationships with 'progressive' notions of schooling and individual development, an idealist conception of history and rational liberal ideology. Jenkins' succinct critique of the empiricist mistrust of empathy and of imagination, arguing that such mistrust rests on highly conservative models of knowledge and schooling, is much stronger. On this see R. Skidelsky (1988b) History as social engineering, *The Independent*, 1 March 1988. Ann Low-Beer (1989) Empathy and history. *Teaching History*, 55, argues that empathy is at most a process in the making of 'historical knowledge and understanding' and that if divorced from these elements it is subject to 'manipulation and rote-learnt' responses. More generally, Jenkins' arguments about empathy are presented separately from his discussion of post-modern analyses of history, and tend to rest on a philosophically, rather than historically grounded analysis of 'understanding other minds' (see note 3). Hilary Cooper, summarizing recent psychological research and research into pupils' historical thinking argues that 'children . . . can make suppositions about how people in the past may have felt and thought [but] . . . this research has been concerned with motives and actions and has not investigated how children may make suppositions about evidence, artefacts, oral evidence, pictures or archaeological sites in order to understand the thoughts and feelings of people who made and used them'. See H. Cooper (1992) *The Teaching of History*, pp. 22–4. London: David Fulton.

3 On post-modern conceptions of history, see Hayden White (1978) *Tropics of Discourse*. Baltimore: Johns Hopkins Press, especially pp. 46–7. See also H. White (1987) *The Content of the Form*, p. 57. Baltimore: Johns Hopkins Press. White's argument is extended and developed by Jenkins, op. cit., especially pp. 33–47, a passage which I find helpful and thought-provoking. The notion of the 'myth of realism' is advanced by Dominic La Capra (1985) *History and Criticism*, pp. 15–44. Ithaca, New York: Cornell University Press. My own

analysis of 'fictions' in history owes a great deal to Peter Burke (1992) *History and Social Theory*, pp. 126–9. Oxford: Polity Press.

4 The stories of Martin Guerre are in Janet Lewis (1969 edition) *The Wife of Martin Guerre*. London: Rapp and Carroll, and Natalie Zemon Davies (1973) *The Return of Martin Guerre*. Cambridge, Massachusetts: Harvard University Press. Davies' interpretation is queried in R. Finlay (1988) The refashioning of Martin Guerre. *American Historical Review*, 93: 553–74, who argues that since Davies acknowledges that her arguments depend on 'omissions' from the sources, they are by definition untestable. For the use of fictions in historical analysis, see Natalie Zemon Davies (1987) *Fiction in the Archives*, pp. 4–5. Oxford: Polity Press.

5 On history, memory and imagination, see Penelope Lively (1978) Children and the art of memory. *Horn Book Magazine*, 54: 197–203; and for an account of ways of thinking about the relationship between the past and (fictional) present, see especially her 1979 *Treasures of Time*. London: Heinemann. On the possibility of imaginative 'truth' in historical novels, see Herbert Butterfield (1924) *The Historical Novel: an essay*, pp. 22–3. Cambridge: Cambridge University Press.

6 R.G. Collingwood (1939) *An Autobiography*. Oxford: University Press. See especially Chapter 2. I owe a great deal to my former colleague Bev Labbett for numerous, always helpful, discussions of Collingwood.

7 R.W. Southern (1977) The historical experience (Rede Lecture, 1977), *Times Literary Supplement*, 24 June 1977, pp. 771–3, quoted in David Lowenthal (1985) *The Past is Another Country*, p. 212. Cambridge: Cambridge University Press.

8 J. Vansina (1974) The power of systematic doubt in historical enquiry. *History in Africa*, 1(1): 109–27; J.H. Hexter (1972) *The History Primer*, pp. 95–8. London: Penguin.

9 E.H. Carr (1961) *What is History?*, pp. 28–30. London: Penguin. See also D. LaCapra (1983) *Rethinking Intellectual History: texts, contexts, language*, p. 17. Ithaca, New York: Cornell University Press.

10 Mark Bevir (1994) Objectivity in history. *History and Theory*, 34(3): 328–44. Bevir's argument, which I find generally convincing and lucid, is that it is indeed impossible to discriminate between accounts of the past taking as his starting point Foucault's contention that 'we do not have access to a given past' and that the objects of historical 'knowledge do not have stable meanings' (see pp. 328–30). It is, however, possible to make judgements between 'webs of interpretation of the past' using 'criteria of comparison': 'because we should respect established standards of evidence and reason, we will prefer webs of interpretations that are accurate, comprehensive and consistent [close fit to most of the agreed facts without contravening principles of logic]. . . . Because we should favour positive speculative theories to those merely blocking criticism, we will prefer webs that

are progressive, fruitful and open [permitting the generation of new ideas and clear about their assumptions so that they facilitate criticism]. . . . We cannot evaluate interpretations definitively or instantly . . . because objectivity rests on *criteria of comparison* [emphasis added]. . . . Historians make sense of the past as best they can; they do not discover certainties' (p. 336, sections in brackets drawn from elsewhere in Bevir's text). Bevir offers a lucid example drawn from discussions in the history of political thought. He argues that the 'webs of interpretation' which history generates are not simply self-referencing because our relationship with the world around us provides an empirical check. We cannot check out *particular* [emphasis added] facts or instances but we can compare 'webs of interpretation'. See also Michael Shanks (1991) *Experiencing the Past: on the character of archaeology*, pp. 39–44, London: Routledge, where a case is made for viewing archaeological reconstruction as the development of 'webs of interpretation'.

11 E.P. Thompson (1978) *The Poverty of Theory*, p. 236. London: Merlin, John Slater [see note 1] suggests that empathy 'enable[s] us to ask questions of current social . . . importance', and concludes that 'sometimes we must keep at arm's length the misleading metaphor of 'balance' (op. cit., pp. 7, 11). On Holocaust education, see the conclusions of M.S. Strom and W.S. Parsons (1982) *Facing History and Ourselves: holocaust and human behaviour*, p. 11, New York: International Education, quoting a student: 'once a person has . . . [studied this] . . . they can never again feel the same way about their humanity or that of others'.

PART TWO

HISTORY IN THE CLASSROOM

HAROLD BRIDGES LIBRARY
S. MARTIN'S COLLEGE
LANCASTER

Miss Lavenham wrote names and dates on the board and we copied them down. We also, to her dictation, noted the principal characteristic of each reign. Henry VIII was condemned by his marital excesses, but was also no good as a king. Queen Elizabeth was good; she fended off the Spaniards and ruled firmly. She also cut off the head of Mary Queen of Scots, who was a Catholic. Our pens scratched in the long summer afternoon. I put up my hand.

'Please, Miss Lavenham, did the Catholics think she was right to cut off Mary's head?'

'No, Claudia, I don't expect they did'.

'Please, do Catholic people think so now?'

Miss Lavenham took a deep breath. 'Well, Claudia,' she said kindly, 'I suppose some of them might not. People do sometimes disagree. But there is no need for you to worry about that. Just put down what is on the board. Make your headings nice and clear in red ink.'

And suddenly for me the uniform grey pond of history is rent; it is fractured into a thousand contending waves; I hear the babble of voices. I put my pen down and ponder; my headings are not nice and clear in red ink. I get 38% (Fail) in the end of term exams.

Penelope Lively (1987) *Moontiger*
London: André Deutsch.

In Chapters 6–9 we will explore some of the implications for the classroom of the interpretive model of history outlined so far. In particular, some of the processes which teachers and pupils might engage in as part of the process of developing understandings of the past will be set out.

Chapter 6 looks at some of the reasons which explain why pupils misunderstand the past, and starts to suggest a way in which we can use initial perceptions as a way of stimulating their learning about history. The next three chapters look in turn at ways of talking, styles of writing and the exercise of judgement about pupils' work. They are presented in this order because they try to describe a process which underpins work in the classroom, centred around the generation of classroom history. Chapter 7 looks at teacher talk and pupil talk. It emphasizes the role of talk in developing understandings and knowledge in the classroom and the interrelationship of teacher talk and pupil talk. Chapter 8 looks at the role of writing and reviews some of the work done over the last twenty years on writing across the curriculum and develops from this a specific model of writing for the history classroom. Chapter 9 looks at judgements, or assessment and considers the relationship between pupil thinking and teacher responses.

Chapter 6

Understandings and misunderstandings

Why do we understand the past differently? Why do pupils misunderstand the purposes of the activities we set them? What are the implications for their classroom learning? Consider these scenarios.

My lesson is about living and working conditions in Manchester in the Industrial Revolution, and I want to explore some of the reasons for inadequate housing, for overcrowding and disease in early industrial towns. I want to explore the reasons for the migration of workers to towns, and the nature of the urban experience in the 1830s. My pupils interpret the evidence I present to them almost solely in terms of the relationships between family members in exclusively twentieth century terms: emotions are run of the mill and pupils seem only to back-project their own understandings of family, of entertainment, or housing.

My lesson is about the beliefs of the Aztecs, and I have spent some time discussing Aztec beliefs and religious practice, but my pupils can only see the funny clothes the Aztecs wore, and they regard the Aztecs as being stupid for holding the beliefs they did.

My lesson is about the Terror in 1790's France, and David's picture sets the events as a cartoon against a suburban landscape of neat semi-detached houses (Figure 6.1).

One reason for understanding the past differently is that the established expectations of history teaching are very influential: the emphasis on 'hard' understandings, on the accumulation of secure historical knowledge about 'where', 'when' and with what proximate causes 'things' happened, in what 'sequence' and with what conferred social 'meaning' that it is easy to neglect the

Figure 6.1 Interpretation of the Terror in 1790s' France.

equally important process by which learners come to under-standings of new contexts and material. Of course 'hard' accumu-lations of knowledge – the 'facts' – have a central role in the development of historical understandings, but they will make little sense unless we examine the ways in which learners appreciate them. If we have learnt a great deal about pupils' historical thinking in the last three decades from the work of the Schools' Council History Project, and from the researches, notably, of Martin Booth, Denis Shemilt, Peter Lee, Alaric Dickinson and Hilary Cooper, it is nonetheless also the case that we have continued in many classrooms to be concerned that pupils are taught – and can then in some context make use of – the correct, or socially approved answer. But the process is, of course, rather more complex: the relationships between new material, our interpretations of it, and the learners' perceptions need to be unpacked rather more carefully.[1]

Ways of thinking about the past: adults and historians

These relationships are a problem not just for pupils in schools, but for all adults attempting to understand the past. No-one ever comes wholly fresh to thinking about the historical past: we all draw on memories, stories, myths, relics, and assumptions of one kind or another in our images of the historical past. When we try to make sense of this historical past, we generally have ideas about the relationship between our contemporary concerns and the past. This relationship is addressed through a range of idiomatic phrases: 'Things aren't what they used to be'; 'You don't know how lucky you are'; 'Things never change, really': all of these summarize popular, widespread and conflicting ideas about what Bob West has called '"the past" with its sinister inverted commas'.[2] Whether our preconceptions are based on ideas of rise or decline, of 'heritage' or 'exploitation', of progress or regress, of change or of stability, they shape powerfully the way we think about the past.

The notion that our interpretations of what we find are not simply derived from our perception is scarcely new, and ex-amples abound in the historiography of the last century or so. The 'invention' of the concept of 'primitive societies' is one example. At the end of the nineteenth century, the concept of primitive society was elaborated by the founders of modern social anthropology: primitive society was based on family groups, which evolved into patrilineal organizations, until territorial ties replaced blood ties as the basis of the community and the state became established as a typical form of social organization. The model was adapted by fieldworker after fieldworker, who either represented 'his' study areas as an illustration of the model or a variant upon it. Marx and Engels adapted the ideas of the model for their own views of the development of human society, and through this route the notion of *primitive society* influenced perhaps eighty years' worth of Marxist history. But the model did not come from observation, or fieldwork in the first place. Its origin is quite clear. Darwin's *The Origins of Species* was published in 1859 and spawned interest in evolutionary models of sociology and history. Within the next twenty years, a succession of 'sociological' monographs 'demonstrated' the evolution of primitive societies. Yet there is scarcely any evidence to support the model of 'primitive society' at all; instead, the adoption of the model by generations of anthropologists became self-fulfilling. They approached remote peoples with an assumption that they were about to find examples of primitive societies, and proceeded to interpret all that they saw in this light.

A second, related example comes from social history concerning the fate of the English peasantry. The notion of a medieval English society as a closed, rural, small-scale stable and intensely local society inhabited by lords and peasants has been a staple of textbook accounts of the Middle Ages for a century. Different historians have variously dated the decline of peasant society and the rise of a 'modern' one to the fifteenth, sixteenth, later seventeenth and later eighteenth centuries. Again, scholars were influenced by strongly evolutionary models of social change which led them to feel that there must have been a transition from 'traditional' to 'modern' society if only they could date it. In the last twenty-five years historians have begun to examine the demographic patterns and social structure of local communities in England between the fourteenth and eighteenth centuries using different models, and have begun to suggest not that peasant society declined but that describing England in the classic terms of a peasant society is simply inappropriate: the description was wrong because the model was wrong.[3]

Some of the ideas which shape the way we look at the past have clear intellectual lineages. Others come from the remotest and deepest sources of our individual experience; they crowd in on us involuntarily. One way of interpreting these assumptions is through the perspective of gestalt psychology, which has drawn our attention to the ways in which our brains see not what is actually 'there' but what they are expecting to see. Certainly this is an important element in the ways in which we make sense of social settings in the past. But there is another. In his celebrated essay on French folk tales, Robert Darnton reviews the ways in which commentators in a psychoanalytic tradition interpreted the traditional peasant story of Red Riding Hood through its 'symbolic language' as a riddle about an adolescent's confrontation with adult sexuality. His conclusion about these interpretations is stark:[4]

> How could anyone get a text so wrong? The difficulty does not derive from professional dogmatism – for psychoanalysts need not be more rigid than poets in their manipulation of symbols – but rather from blindness to the historical dimension.

Ways of seeing the past: pupils and learners

This sense of 'blindness to the historical dimension' is of considerable importance in the teaching of history in schools. The complication arrives from attempts to disentangle two aspects of our understandings of the past. On the one hand, the past was different from the present (in its social arrangements, ways of belief, forms of relationships) but at the same time people in the past were like us (they became hungry, they slept, they were ill, they grieved, they worried, they feasted, they went hungry, they rejoiced, they were sad). Teachers have a number of ways of describing and responding to their pupils' misunderstandings and misconceptions, though such misunderstandings seem peculiarly persistent and resistant to change. One not unusual response is to dismiss them as 'unhistorical'; they are produced by pupils who lack a sense of period, who fail both to think in appropriate ways about the evidence presented to them or to consider elementary ideas about the differences between ourselves and the past. The most notable description of the problem comes from the work of Peter Lee and Rosalyn Ashby, who characterize the unhistoricality of some pupils' views in this way (Figure 6.2):

Figure 6.2   A model of cognitive development in terms of pupils' ability to understand behaviours and beliefs in the past. Examples are drawn from Anglo-Saxon trials.

Stage 1: The 'divi' past
'That sort of thing we wouldn't be doing nowadays 'cos we're not that stupid nowadays.'

Stage 2: The stereotyped past
'The difference is . . . that they believe in God and we don't believe in God but they . . . believe that God does everything like.'

Stage 3: Every day understandings
'If I was . . . an old farmer and people took my land, I'd be very upset and I'd really try to get it back, but . . . I wouldn't have any chance I reckon, 'cos, say if a rich person took it, like I said before, they can give plenty of money to say "This is my land" and they can buy land and everything and, I just, I think that's not right.'

Stage 4: Restricted historical understanding
'If he is accepted as innocent by God, and then, then he's, when he's thrown into the hole filled with water, he'd sink lower than the two metres, but if he's proved, um, guilty by God, then he won't sink lower.'

Stage 5: Contextualized historical understanding
'Although they were probably intelligent, they probably didn't have the . . . they believed in God of course . . . so they thought if God's so clever and powerful we'll let him do the judging and we'll carry out the punishments if need be . . . the system was as fair as the current culture would allow.'

Categories are based on, and pupil quotations drawn from P. Lee and R. Ashby (1987) Children's concepts of empathy and understanding in history in C. Portal (ed.) *The History Curriculum for Teachers*, pp. 68–86. Falmer: Lewes.

People in the past were in an important way, mentally defective ('divi', 'thick') because they failed to adopt obviously 'better' courses of action. . . . The real basis of this is the inability of the pupil to recognise that people in the past often could not know – either in general or in the details of the situation in which they were called upon to act – what the pupil now knows and takes for granted. Add to this the pupil's inability to envisage the inherent complexity of human institutions and interactions and the past becomes a catalogue of absurd behaviour to which the only possible reaction is one of irritated incomprehension and contempt.[5]

This failure to comprehend the ways in which the past was different from the present – the failure to grasp the nature of historical context – is an important source of pupil misunderstanding. It means that pupils find it difficult to consider the reasons for, or even the nature of historical change in any way other than simply the passing of time: the past was simply a pre-existing 'present'. Another parallel type of misunderstanding arises from pupils' failure to identify the ways in which people in the past were similar to us. Sometimes, pupils fail to grasp historical actors' intentions in choosing a particular course of action. Sometimes, they are unable, by virtue of their immature grasp of human motivation, to see underlying causal connections between different actions and events. In other cases, they lack a historical frame of reference so that they are unable to locate individual actions and events in the range of possible actions, or beliefs available to historical actors. Greater pupil sophistication in acquiring and communicating historical understanding is then a consequence both of wider exposure to different models of causal connection in history – understanding, for example, that events had multiple causes or varying importance, or had different social, economic, political and religious causes, or had interconnected causes – but also of an increasing emotional and moral sophistication.

How can we address these misconceptions, misapprehensions and misunderstandings? How can we support pupils' learning about the past in ways which both open their minds to the ways in which the past was different from the present and allow them to adjust their views of themselves and of how people think and live so that new perceptions are incorporated into their revised thinking. It is useful to think about the way in which historical understanding might develop by using the similarity/difference model, but it may not be entirely helpful in demonstrating how we can work with pupils in classrooms to develop more sophisticated sorts of historical thinking and understanding. Cognitive psychologists have pointed out that an enormous proportion of children's learning has already occurred before they enter formal schooling: their use of language, their understandings of themselves and their world is already highly advanced by the time they reach the age of five. Pupils do not come into school as 'empty vessels'. They bring into school, and into the history classroom, their own ideas about their own world, their knowledge, understandings and, as important, misunderstandings about the societies they are learning about, and a set of more general assumptions about the way people behave. This is true even of very young children. The ideas that young people have about their world and the worlds of the past have a number of fairly obvious characteristics; their understandings are local, personalized and fragmentary. Their sense of time is restricted. To different degrees, this is as true of a teenager as it is of a five- or six-year old: the difference is likely to lie in the sort of historical or human issues with which we confront them in the classroom. They apply ideas about their own experience to the past intermittently, and they offer explanations of other places or periods in ways which sometimes relate to their own experience and sometimes not.

Minitheories and understanding the past

Guy Claxton has described this sort of behaviour as the application of what he calls 'minitheories'. Minitheories provide learners with ways of explaining aspects of the world: they are fragmentary and often contradictory. Claxton divides minitheories in the context of school science into three categories – what he calls 'gut', 'lay' and 'school science'. Gut minitheories are based on unarticulated reactions to experiences. Much instinctive reaction to experiences is of this sort – 'I don't like it', 'The object is ugly', 'The picture is beautiful', 'The man was stupid'. Lay minitheories are derived from those with whom children come into contact, from the media, from books. Children collect a huge number of understandings of the past from the world around them. On the London Underground, an advertisement for the Tower of London pictures Henry VIII asking for 'A return to the Tower and a single for the wife'. On Christmas cards, in fairy tales, in costume dramas there are portrayals of an imagined past which powerfully influences children's constructions of the past: a past of stagecoaches and gaslights, of castles and kings. In picture books, the past is represented through often sharply, sometimes crudely, drawn stereotypes: the king and the queen at their court, typically a semi-medieval sort of court. In western movies, there are portrayals of native Americans, of cowboys and gunfights which contribute to images of 'the West' and the 'Indian' long before pupils encounter these images in the classroom.

All this means that pupils acquire minitheories about the past about how people lived in the past and about the way they organized their relationships with each other in the past from a bewildering variety of sources. Onto these minitheories we graft – in relatively small units of time in school – images and understandings of the past which are based on acquiring and processing information within academic canons of reliability, explanation and justification. How does this formal learning relate to the minitheories pupils already have? Claxton concludes his argument about learning and minitheories by observing that:

> on the minitheory view there are two main types of
> learning: that which involves modification of existing
> modules [of explanation], and that which involves the
> creation of a new, purpose-built minitheory to deal with a
> new domain of experience . . . [A third possibility] is
> restructuring the existing gut/lay minitheory so that a full
> understanding and resolution of the conflict results.[6]

In the history classroom, we are concerned both with the modification of existing explanations through refinement and with the creation of new, restructured meanings, both with asking pupils to acquire information and to solve problems. Pupils' gut and lay minitheories overlap: they have seen a western movie which tells them some things about the native American, but they also draw on their ideas about motivation to explain individual behaviours. If we are examining with pupils the reasons for prolonged sectarian rivalry in Northern Ireland, we need both to refine understanding by examining individual incidents – the Act of Union in 1800, the partition of 1920, the civil rights demonstrations of the later 1960s, Bloody Sunday, the Anglo-Irish agreement of 1985 – and to restructure their understanding of motivation so that they understand why these events acquired the significance they did with different communities. If we are looking at the execution of Louis XVI in 1793 we can do so both through the sequence of events which led to the execution, but understanding will depend on extending pupils' grasp of people's ideas and beliefs in the French Revolution. In helping pupils to understand why it was that white Americans in the nineteenth century were unable to reach a lasting accommodation with native Americans we need not only to look at the Indian Wars, but to shift pupils' sense of the sharply contrasting ideas native Americans had about the nature of land and its ownership. In all these cases, the encounter with the past is both an encounter with events, objects, evidence and an encounter with abstract ideas: at some point the learner has to unlock relationships between them if he or she is to adapt, or restructure one of her minitheories through this encounter with the past.

Reshaping minitheories: museum education

These relationships are, perhaps, particularly sharply focused in museums. Museum educators have begun to address the ways in which coherent knowledge about the past is shaped in museum collections, and their work is instructive for work in classrooms. In museums, we encounter the past through its material remains. Museums provide material testimony about the past, but the past, and understandings of it, are not contained in museums: we build interpretations from the objects, from the ways in which they are juxtaposed on display, from the ways in which they are labelled and from the ways we interpret what we see, which in turn depends on the ideas about the past and its remains which we already have. Building interpretations of the past depends on linking what we see to what we already think about the past, to the ideas we, and our children, bring into the museum. Understanding depends on something more, on linking what is displayed to the past to which it refers and from which it is separated. So understanding the past represented in the museum collection depends on the active involvement of the learner – on the deployment by the learner of the minitheories he or she brings to the museum. For this reason, the strategies of museum educators are important clues for us in thinking about the place of learners in understanding the past. Frances Sword notes that:

> . . . the functions of many objects are multi-faceted and complex. An Egyptian coffin, for example, was made to hold not just a body but a belief system: the body was contained in the coffin, and the belief system is contained in its style. The object contains many sorts of information but, as with so many artefacts style is the thickest cable of communication. . . . Whatever the object, if it communicates through its style, we are presented with ideas held in shape, form and colour which are often far more important than those held by any other aspect of the artefacts. In order for children to reach this rich area of information I believe it necessary for us to think creatively about use of language.

Sword then goes on to highlight the critical importance of providing opportunities for learners to explore the ideas they bring to the galleries:

> . . . If we are primarily interested in learning, we must create situations where children's own perceptions become the steps up which they climb.[7]

This is a powerful image: seeing our own perceptions in new ways is one of the most powerful ways of developing new ideas. In this sense, what we see as 'misunderstandings' can, from the perspective of minitheories and ladders of perception, be elements in the development of higher level understandings. How can we create situations where pupils' perceptions become ladders which permit the development of new learning rather than prisons which confine and limit their own understanding? How, to put it differently, can we ensure that pupil misunderstandings become the basis for the development of understandings? Time is always at a premium in schools and classrooms, and it may appear to be perfect counsel to suggest that the starting point for classroom work needs to be explicit opportunities for pupils to explore and examine the 'minitheories' they bring to new historical problems. However, Ashby and Lee conclude their discussion of pupils' conceptions of understanding in history by commenting that:

> . . . it is possible to spend time discovering how children see things, without feeling guilty that too little ground is being covered. In the end it is more interesting listening to pupils and trying to understand why they see things as they do than it is to hear one's own voice trying to push them into giving the wrong answer.[8]

In classrooms, much of the work in which pupils engage asks them to focus their own personal reaction to new stimuli: to new evidence, to new problems, to new texts, to new questions. This personal reaction is important, but since learners will always react to new material using the minitheories they already deploy, it needs to be supplemented by something else if pupils are to climb the ladder of their own perceptions to generate new understandings of the past. The power of talk and language is well documented, but the real power resides in opportunities to pool ideas and share insights in small 'intimate' groups, to explore one's own perceptions and minitheories in detail before being asked to deploy and defend ideas, insights or understandings in formal, or plenary settings.[9]

Minitheories and interpretations of history

We have now discussed the ways in which we describe the relationship between pupils and the historical material, the ideas, evidence, language and information, with which they are confronted in classrooms. Pupils' ideas about the past are linked to the ideas they already have about human motivation, to the experiences and ideas they bring into school and they can be located in a host of sources out of school. Pupils interpret the material they encounter in school in terms of the minitheories which they bring to this material. In classrooms, we need to help them:

- to extend, to enrich or to refine these minitheories: to extend and deepen, for example, their grasp of international rivalry before the First World War in order to widen their understanding of the causes of the First World War;

- to restructure their understanding of causation – for example to understand that the proximate cause is not necessarily the most significant element; and
- to provide interpretive statements about the past in which pupils make their own assumptions explicit rather than simply subsuming their assumptions in the material they are analysing.

The argument is that we will find it profitable to think of this encounter with the past in terms of an attempt on our part to generate in pupils *webs of interpretation*. The task of the history teacher is to stimulate the development of these webs of interpretation by providing opportunities for pupils to develop new ways of thinking based around new ways of seeing issues and, importantly, new ways of talking about them.

Notes

1 On the subject of research into pupils' cognitive development in history, the influence of Piaget's cognitive frameworks on thinking about history was strongest in the 1960s, since when researchers have generally argued that they have little utility in analysing the ways in which pupils construct understandings of the past. The Schools Council History Project (1972–76) argued that whilst there is 'no body of knowledge with a coherent structure in history', nonetheless 'much can be done . . . to develop pupils' conceptual understanding of what history involves by giving children the opportunity of handling and using historical evidence'. The Project's argument that 'history involves some attempt to re-think the past' led to an emphasis on the use of evidence and the application of judgement in the classroom. See Schools Council (1976) *A New Look at History*, pp. 10, 17–18. Edinburgh: Holmes McDougall. The Project's work was paralleled by, and stimulated, considerable research into pupils' historical thinking. Martin Booth's work with adolescents led him to argue that 14–16-year-old pupils are capable of construing the past in a genuinely historical manner provided that they are taught in ways which emphasize the uniqueness of history and in ways which provide opportunities for interpretive work. 'Adductive historical thinking' which Booth observed among his study cohort appeared to depend on the acquisition of relevant factual knowledge, analytical and conceptual ability, attitudes towards the subject, personal experiences and verbal abilities. See M. Booth (1979) A longitudinal study of cognitive skills, concepts and attitudes of adolescents studying a modern world

history syllabus and an analysis of their adductive historical thinking. Unpublished PhD thesis, Reading University. Booth's ideas are developed in M. Booth (1987) Ages and concepts: a critique of the Piagetian approach to history teaching in C. Portal (ed.) *The History Curriculum for Teachers*, pp. 22–38. Lewes: Falmer, where Booth argues for pupils' ability, given open-ended learning activities, to 'get to grips with complex, abstract ideas' (p. 38). Denis Shemilt's evaluation of the Schools Council History Project led him to propose a series of stage models for the development of various strands of historical thinking, although he argued that these were not strictly age-related Piagetian constructs. See Denis Shemilt (1983) The devil's locomotive. *History and Theory*, 22: 1–18. For discussion of pupils' understanding of human motivations, see A.K. Dickinson and P.J. Lee (1978) Understanding and research in A.K. Dickinson and P.J. Lee (eds) *History Teaching and Historical Understanding*, pp. 94–120. London: Heinemann. On younger children's ideas about the past, Hilary Cooper (1995) *History in the Early Years*, pp. 17–21. London: Routledge, shows the ways in which pupils construct models of the past through play.

2 On popular representations of the past, the 'heritage' industry has been analysed from a number of critical perspectives. The quotation is from Bob West (1988) The making of the English working past: a critical view of the Ironbridge Gorge Museum in R. Lumley (ed.) *The Museum Time Machine*, p. 17. London: Routledge. See also Patrick Wright's arguments about the creation of a myth of 'deep England' set out in his 1985 *On Living in an Old Country*. London: Verso. By contrast, Nick Merriman's research into popular ideas about the past amongst museum visitors suggests that most people have very negative images of the past and believe very strongly in linear progressions from a past of poverty, deprivation and ill health: N. Merriman (1991) *Beyond the Glass Case*, pp. 20, 29, 35. Leicester: Leicester University Press.

3 On historians' preconceptions about the past, for an account of the development of the idea of 'primitive society', see A. Kuper (1988) *The Invention of Primitive Society*, pp. 5–7, 64–72, 231–5. London and New York: Routledge. The example of the Tiv people in central Nigeria is particularly instructive. They had a reputation with the British administrator for lawless anarchy, and in 1907 the British resident C.F. Gordon analysed the clan structure of the Tiv. A decade later an overstretched British administration found it convenient to bracket the Tiv with their more numerous neighbours, the Hausa. Obligingly, Tiv headmen began to speak Hausa, dress like Hausa and so on. In 1930, the Tiv were visited by R.C. Abraham, a government anthropologist and R.O. Downes, a District Officer, at the time when British administration was working towards a model of 'native' administration based on indirect rule. Their report urged the government to encourage the role of Tiv paramount chiefs who could lead local

councils. By 1940, a further report noted that there was evidence that the Tiv were ruled by patriarchs who formed a pyramid of authority! We know this largely through the work of a historian who realized that the investigators were interactively part of the history they produced. See D.C. Dorwald (1974) Ethnography and administration: the study of Anglo-Tiv 'working misunderstanding'. *Journal of African History*, 15: 457–77. I owe this example to Gwyn Prins (1992) Oral History in P. Burke (ed.) *New Perspectives on Historical Writing*, pp. 123–6. Oxford: Blackwell. The example of the idea of the decline of English peasant society is best, if controversially, set out in Alan Macfarlane (1978) *The Origins of English Individualism*. Oxford: Blackwell. The power of evolutionary models of thinking is lucidly explored by Stephen Jay Gould (1990) *Wonderful Life: the Burgess Shale and the Nature of History*, ch. 1. New York: Hutchinson.

4 David Lowenthal sets out the ways in which our sense of the past develops through memory, chronicle and history in D. Lowenthal (1985) *The Past is a Foreign Country* pp. 202–3. Cambridge: University Press. For psychoanalytic interpretations of folk tales, see Robert Darnton (1984) Peasants tell tales in *The Great Cat Massacre*, p. 11. New York: Basic Books.

5 The 'divi past' and progression in learning are to be found in P. Lee and R. Ashby (1987) Children's concepts of empathy and understanding in history in C. Portal (ed.) *The History Curriculum for Teachers*, p. 68. Lewes: Falmer.

6 On minitheories, see G. Claxton (1993) Minitheories: a preliminary model for learning science in P.J. Black and A.M. Lucas (eds) *Children's Informal Ideas in Science*, pp. 45–61. London: Routledge.

7 On learning in museums, Frances Sword (1994) Points of contact. *Journal of Education in Museums*, 15: 7–9 is the source of the quotation; Frances Sword is an outstanding museum educator. On the way in which perception, museum settings and understanding intertwine more generally, see C. Husbands (1992a) Objects and interpretations in museum education. *Journal of Education in Museums*, 13: 1–3. Ideas about the way in which museum exhibits are read and explored by Pauline McManus (1991) 'Making sense of exhibits' and by E. Hooper-Greenhill (1991) 'A new communication model for museums', both in S. Pearce (ed.) *Museum Languages: objects and texts*. Leicester: Leicester University Press. Both set out a model of communication in which the museum visitor plays an active role in the construction of 'meanings' and 'understandings'. For an outstanding example of the way in which this has worked with pupils with severe learning difficulties, see A. Pearson and C. Aloysius (1994) *The Big Foot: museums and children with learning difficulties*. London: British Museum Press.

8 P. Lee and R. Ashby, op. cit., p. 86.

9 On the power of types of talk, see Chapter 7.

Ways of talking: words, classrooms and history

Most history teaching takes place in less than ideal circumstances: we teach in classrooms with rows of desks, or groups of tables, classrooms which are invariably too hot in summer and cold in winter, classrooms which are stuffy, which may leak, and which show the wear and tear of years of adolescents sloping in and rushing out. We share rooms with other teachers, and we lack storage space in the rooms we have for ourselves. We use teaching materials which are dog-eared and sometimes defaced, and we have inadequate display spaces for pupils' work and inadequate time to use what we do have effectively. And from these unpromising surroundings we seek to create, or recreate the illusion that this is not a hot classroom with a distracted class who have just come from Technology or PE, not a draughty classroom in the final lesson on a Friday afternoon, but that the classroom is an archive of evidence, from which we can glean nuggets of information which will allow us to speculate, hypothesize about the past we are describing; that the classroom is a Roman villa, a Saxon hut, an Aztec temple, an international conference hall or a slave plantation. Of course, the classroom cannot *become* any of these things; it remains a classroom, but if we are trying with our pupils to *reconstruct*, to *understand* the past and its populations, the classroom is a particularly inhospitable setting: it lacks the colour of the theatre, the dusty atmosphere of the archive or the architectural brilliance of the castle. This means that the principal teaching tools we have to develop our pupils' understanding and awareness are words: their words, our words and the words of actors in the past as they are presented to us in documents, or as textbook accounts. The way in which we use language and the opportunities we create for our pupils to use language will largely shape the way in which they think about the past. If the classroom can support historical thinking and historical understanding, it will be through the language we employ about the past in its setting more than through the setting itself.

It has been suggested that historical language is an interpretive web through which we construct our interpretations of the past and that historical evidence provides above all else a series of springboards for pupils to think about the past. What are the implications for communication in the classroom of the sort of historical thinking which I have been sketching in Chapters 2 to 6? One way of exploring this is to begin by looking at the activity which occupies substantial parts of classroom time: talking. Teachers talk to their pupils; they use talk to exercise control, to organize their pupils around administrative tasks, to introduce new historical material, to set written or oral or dramatic tasks, to encourage or to correct pupils, to tell stories, to describe historical sources, to situate historical examples in a wider historical frame of reference, to bring lessons to an end, to connect lessons together in a sequence. The language teachers use, and the ways in which they deploy it in history lessons is an important element in the sort of learning activities which go on and the sort of understandings which pupils accumulate. Pupils talk in lessons too. They talk in response to teacher questions, they talk to each other in small groups, collaborative learning, they talk out loud in class discussions or role-playing presentations to their peers. Frequently, their talk is unplanned, spontaneous and instinctive; sometimes it is closely related to the task we have set them, but sometimes it is not. Pupil talk and teacher talk are essential ingredients of the generation of historical knowledge in the history classroom. How can we most effectively use talk in the generation of interpretive understandings in history?[1]

Teachers, talk and communicating history

There are conventional models of teacher talk in the history classroom: the job of the history teacher is to 'teach' pupils history by 'describing' the past in 'appropriate' language. The 'outcome' of such teaching is that teachers will have 'transmitted' to their pupils 'knowledge' about the past. This rather caricatured model has been under sustained attack for almost two decades, but it exerts a powerful cultural hold on teachers and on classrooms. The weaknesses of the argument for transmission models of teaching are by now well-known, largely through the work of Douglas Barnes and more recently through the work of Alan Howe and the National Oracy Project.[2] In transmission models of teaching, there are fundamental difficulties in choosing language appropriate to the linguistic development of the learners; in transmission models of teaching, we tend to focus on the outcomes for which we strive rather than the processes by which learners acquire their understandings. Transmission models of history teaching understate the knowledge, understandings and 'minitheories' which, we have seen, even very young children bring into school with them. On the interpretive model of history outlined, transmission models of teaching neglect the place of interpretive understandings which lie at the core of the development of historical knowledge.

For these reasons and others, there has been a severe reaction to the model of teacher talk which underpins transmission approaches in history. Emphasis has been placed on developing classroom methodologies which encourage pupils to develop their learning through the active use of language rather than through listening and writing. For one commentator:

> My own observations push forward a stark and slightly
> frightening conclusion: that teacher talk may well be
> largely irrelevant in the history classroom.[3]

The aim here is not to take issue with the fundamental critique of transmission-based models of teaching in history lessons but to argue that teacher talk, and the way teachers use language in lessons plays a central role in the way pupils learn. The collection of papers on the National Oracy Project outlines a variety of ways in which teacher talk can stimulate pupil learning (see Table 7.1), and indicates a critical role for the teacher in what is described as scaffolding learning and supporting the generation of a 'pupil agenda'.

Teachers 'scaffold' pupil learning in history when they draw on their experience, education and training to support the ways in which they wish pupils to think about historical issues. Teachers,

Table 7.1 Learning through talking and the role of the teacher: insights from the National Oracy Project

---

Responding to children's expertise
Responding as a working group member
Responding as a neutral chairperson
'Scaffolding' learning
Responding as a source of information
Responding as a learning partner
Responding with minimal intervention

Source: R. Corden (1992) The role of the teacher in K. Norman (ed.) *Thinking Voices: the Work of the National Oracy Project*, pp. 172–84. London: Hodder and Stoughton, for the National Curriculum Council.

by definition, have a wider frame of historical reference than pupils. They have read more widely, are able to make connections between historical issues more confidently, and have a wider perspective on the nature and structure of historical change. This 'expertise' in the nature of the discipline is what they have to contribute to pupils' developing grasp of the subject. The way in which they talk, the way in which they introduce historical issues and the way in which they relate these issues to learners' thinking, is what characterizes their task as a history teacher. But such talk can be overstructured; it can give too much away. The place of story, we have seen, is to *support* pupil thinking, not to replace it. The place of historical problem-setting is to introduce possibilities, not to close them down. The place of teacher talk is to generate *meaning* and *relevance*, to support the ways in which pupils construct interpretive understandings of the past (Table 7.2). When teachers use language in this way, they are not simply deploying effective learning techniques, but are occupying one of the roles which oral historians have highlighted in their analysis of oral traditions as historical process. Jan Vansina has offered an account of the significance of oral tradition as a *historical* source, in which he argues that the communication of messages from one generation to another – which is what happens when teachers talk to their pupils – is neither simply about the transmission of news nor the repetition of tradition but is centrally concerned with the interpretation of experience, which 'involve not only perception but also emotions . . . essential to a notion of personality and identity'. The way

Table 7.2   Teacher talk and the generation of historical understanding

---

The role of the teacher as:
- provider of information
    the storyteller
    the historical context
- interpreter [the teacher as historian]
- organizer of resources and pupils
- questioner using pupils' experiences and ideas
- performer
- power of problems (what if?; how about?; what do *you* think of?)

---

teachers describe the past is a powerful element in the way pupils construct their own images of the past.[4]

Gaining expertise: pupils and talk

When teachers talk in history classrooms they do so from a position of authority: they have the authority which the classroom situation confers on them, and they have the authority which comes from their command of their subject. When pupils talk in history classrooms they generally do so from a position of weakness and disadvantage. They do not know the significance of the information they possess, they generally do not understand how it relates to other ideas and information, and they do not, usually, know where the information and ideas they are using are likely to lead.

Nowhere is this imbalance in relationship more clearly demonstrated than in those occasions where teachers ask questions of classes of pupils. Such questioning plays an enormously significant role in classroom life. One estimate is that teachers can expect, during the course of their teaching career, to ask something in excess of one-and-a-half million questions. Classroom questions *appear* to offer considerable potential: they are occasions in which we pool knowledge, check that information has been accumulated, draw out pupils' own experiences – and so on. But the efficacy of classroom questioning has been seriously questioned by David Wood.[5] Where teachers typically ask something like two questions a minute, pupils rarely ask more than two questions an hour. Where in everyday life we ask questions to elicit information ('Can you tell me the way to . . . ?') teachers ask questions to which they generally already know the answers ('What was the date of the Battle of Hastings?'). Where in normal discourse we would give our interlocutor time to consider the answer to a question, to think through a response, teachers expect speedy responses in order to maintain pace and direction. Where questioning derives from a Socratic ideal in which the teacher asked questions to motivate, sustain enquiry and encourage reflection and analysis, most classroom questioning, in history at least, is concerned with relatively low level matters to do with checking that information has been encountered or work completed. In these situations, questioning appears to lose most of its force, and fits uneasily beside the model of historical understanding outlined so far.

When historians use questioning in their work, they appear to do so rather differently. There are few accounts but in Wineburg's comparison of the ways in which academic historians conducted a historical enquiry with the ways in which school pupils conducted a similar enquiry, for the academic historians:

> Text emerge as 'speech acts', social interactions set down
> on paper that can be understood only by trying to
> reconstruct the social context in which they occurred . . .
> as historical texts become rich and conceptually complex,
> readers may slow down not because they fail to
> comprehend but because the very act of comprehension
> demands that they stop to '*talk*' with their texts.

In the history classroom, too, Levine outlines an aspiration for questioning in which questioning acts as a:

> way for learners to articulate their doubts , or as a means to
> resolve those doubts.[6]

If we are to realize the potential of classroom talk to develop interpretive understandings of the past, then we need to shift the emphasis of classroom questioning in two ways. The first involves a transition from an initial concern with outcomes in teacher questioning to a concern with processes and ideas. Outcomes do of course matter: the understandings which we are attempting to provide opportunities for pupils to develop are concerned with significant issues, and the way they integrate those understandings into models and ideas about the past is a matter of concern for history teachers, a subject returned to in Chapter 9. But it is precisely because outcomes in the form of pupil understanding matter that we have in our classroom questioning to be concerned with the way in which we provide opportunities for pupils to articulate their questions, their doubts and their concerns about the issues we are discussing. It is because outcomes matter that our primary concern in seeking responses to oral questions from classes should be with historical ideas, with the way in which we have asked pupils to learn. We can, in short, draw distinctions between those types of classroom question which are largely about process, about ways of learning and about the ways in which we want pupils to reach interpretive understandings, and those questions which call forth interpretive understandings. And it is the former type which needs to predominate.

The second transition is concerned less with the type of questioning than the way in which it is developed and formulated. Commentators such as Nick Levine and John McGill from the early and mid-1980s have already been quoted, arguing for the deployment of more exploratory talk in history. But neither was able to offer clear and convincing classroom methodologies for such talk. It is a measure of how much we have learnt from the work of the National Oracy Project in the later 1980s and early 1990s that we are now able to think more clearly about creating opportunities for meaningful talk across the curriculum. Where teachers have in the past frequently been sceptical about creating opportunities for productive use of pupils' classroom talk, pupils' words have been shown, under appropriate circumstances to be 'surprisingly disciplined squads'.[7]

If talk is to be productive of learning, pupils need opportunities to explore ideas purposefully in a variety of settings. There are numerous techniques which can be deployed in order to create such opportunities in history (see Figure 7.1). Underpinning all these techniques, however, is a simple model of classroom talk, which identifies three types of opportunity for pupils to formulate and develop their ideas and connects them in a simple sequence: pupils need opportunities to develop ideas in *private*, in *small* groups, and in open *plenary* discussion.[8] None of these opportunities stands alone. It is important that we create space

Figure 7.1 Organizing opportunities for talk in history.

Jigsawing
Students are placed in 'expert' groups which examine different aspects of a given topic. They are then reorganized into home groups so that each home group can draw on the 'expertise' of one of the 'experts'.

Rainbow groups
Groups are asked to discuss different aspects of a topic and are then grouped, by number, into new groups. Each new group is made up of representatives of every original group.

Speaking documents
Pupils are given original or simplified versions of a historical document. They:
● discuss what might have happened before or after the document;
● turn it into a storyboard;
● describe to others in the class what has happened to the document since it was written.

Playing experts
Pupils assume the role of an expert: historian, archaeologist, curator, archivist, etc. They are given a piece of collection of evidence and have to describe how it could be used in an interesting display/reconstruction.

Commentaries
Using newsreel footage without commentary, or photographs or prints pupils must devise a commentary.

Hotseating/character in role
Teacher/child researches a historical figure and is then interviewed by the rest of the class about their actions/beliefs.

Cooperative activity
Any small group activity in which pupils have to *collaborate* to produce a presentation/product.

Based on: A. Howe (1992) *Making Talk Work*, pp. 18–19. London: Hodder and Stoughton. G. Bage (1995) Chaining the Beast: an examination of how the pedagogic use of spoken stories may make historical narrative richer and more susceptible to analysis by children. An autobiographical research study by an advisory teacher. Unpublished PhD thesis, University of East Anglia, Appendix 2.

for pupils to recollect instances or evidence, to develop their ideas and to consider an initial reaction to new ideas, to questions or to new material. This might involve building a 'pause' into questioning, but it could equally involve asking pupils, before they say anything in response to a question to jot down their first thoughts briefly. If we move too quickly from asking pupils to reflect in this way to asking them to present their ideas or to draw their conclusions together, then it is unlikely that they will develop their thinking to any level of sophistication. For this reason, it is just as important that the first excursion for their ideas should, often, be in a small group, pooling initial reactions or early data, exploring their ideas and material in response to a common task. This sort of talk makes the development of ideas, the comparison of different perspectives possible. Finally, pupils will be in a position to contribute to open discussion – to respond to classroom questions – on the basis of information, knowledge and expertise: in other words, from a position of strength rather than disadvantage.

Creating history through talk

Where transmission-derived modes of teaching dominate the history classroom, where history is preconstructed by the textbook or the teacher or the questioning which derives from one or the other, we shall find it difficult to develop in our pupils the interpretive understandings of history which underpinned the earlier chapters of this book. Talk, as John McGill puts it:[9]

> makes possible the restructuring of knowledge: a creative history emerges when pupils are enabled to discuss the whys and wherefores. . . . History teachers need to define what talk is and what it can do in the classroom. . . . Talk can take many forms: it can be a means towards thoughtful use of evidence; it can have an impact on written products; talk can inform teachers about the nature not only of the tasks set but of pupils themselves.

For teachers, this demands a sensitivity to the way their pupils speak and the way they use language themselves in describing and framing activities. It means using the classroom as a place in which language is used to explore ideas and issues rather than simply to describe the 'outcomes' of reading and discussion. It means, in short, emphasizing in all we do the importance of *having ideas* and *exploring ideas* about the past. Words, for both teachers and pupils are the most potentially powerful tool we have in thinking about history.

Notes

1 On the generation of understandings through talk, the most important recent text is D. Edwards and N. Mercer (1992) *Common Knowledge*.
London: Routledge.

2 On the difficulties of 'transmission' models of teaching, the argument
is most clearly advanced by D. Barnes (1976) *From Communication to
Curriculum*. London: Penguin. On the work of the National Oracy
Project, see G. Wells, (1992) The centrality of talk in education in K.
Norman (ed.) *Thinking Voices: the work of the National Oracy Project*,
pp. 283–311. London: Hodder and Stoughton for the National Curriculum Council and A. Howe (1992) *Making Talk Work*. London:
Hodder and Stoughton. On approaches to classroom talk more
generally, see P. Jones (1988) *Lipservice: the story of talk in schools*,
pp. 144–52. Milton Keynes: Open University Press. On the transmission model in history, see David Sylvester's characterization of the
'great tradition' of 'active didacticism' in history teaching in D.
Sylvester (1994) Change and continuity in history teaching, 1900–1993
in H. Bourdillon (ed.) *Teaching History*, pp. 9–25. London: Routledge
for the Open University. For different approaches to the place of talk in
history, see N. Levine (1981) *Language Teaching and Learning: History*,
pp. 52–81. London: Ward Lock.

3 On the subject of alternatives to teacher talk in the history classroom,
the quotation is from J. McGill (1988) In the history classroom in J.
Hickman and K. Kimberley, *Teachers, Language and Learning*, p. 78.
London: Routledge. For a wider critique, see P. Waterhouse (1983)
Managing the Learning Process. London: McGraw-Hill.

4 On historians and oral traditions, the central text is J. Vansina (1987)
Oral Tradition as History, pp. 4, 7–8. Oxford: University Press.

5 On classroom questioning, the paragraph is derived from D. Wood
(1992) Teaching talk: how modes of teacher talk affect pupil participation in K. Norman (ed.) op. cit., pp. 203–6. See also p. 210:
'Questions are not the only, nor are they usually the best, means of
engendering evidence of thought'. On history questions, see P. John
(1994) Academic tasks in history classrooms. *Research in Education*,
51: 11–22.

6 On dialogues between researcher and sources, see S. Wineburg (1991)

On the reading of historical texts: notes on the breach between School and Academy. *American Education Research Journal*, 28(3): 499–515; the quotation is from pp. 500, 503. Also see Pocock, op. cit., p. 161: the historian 'may well end by basing his pattern on a quite limited number of sources, and if he knows how to do it properly he may do more with those sources than sit and read, sit and think, sit and write'. On classrooms, the quotation is drawn from Levine, op. cit., p. 27; cf. McGill, op. cit., p. 79: 'teachers talk too much, students too little'.

7 On oracy, the key texts are Howe, op. cit. and Norman (ed.) op. cit. The phrase quoted is from H. Gardiner (1992) Surprisingly disciplined squads, Norman (ed.) op. cit., pp. 196–202. See also H. Kemeny (1993) (ed.) *Learning Together Through Talk: Key Stages 3 and 4*. London: Hodder and Stoughton for the National Curriculum Project. Also M. McClure, T. Phillips and A. Wilkinson (eds) (1988) *Oracy Matters*. Milton Keynes: Open University Press.

8 I owe this model, and a great deal of my own thinking on classroom talk and language to Mike Hayhoe.

9 On the classroom potential of talk in history, the quotation is from McGill, op. cit., pp. 80–1. See also M.B. Booth (1993) *The Teaching and Learning of History: a British perspective*. Göteborgs Universitet: Projektet Europa och läroboken, where the importance of discussion in the development of adductive thinking is described.

Chapter 8

Organizing ideas: the place of writing

Writing has a central place in classrooms generally and certainly in the learning of history. Pupils spend a substantial part of their time writing. They produce hundreds of thousands of words in exercise books and on file paper during their school career. Frequently, pupils can only discover what they think and what they know by writing. Writing can also allow pupils to work out ideas and can reflect on them, record observations, note, and clarify ideas in order to formulate their own understandings, they make their ideas public to teachers and to their peers. A pupil's formulation of ideas in writing is an individual statement, and a substantial part of a teacher's job is to respond to these written ideas, to make judgements about them and to feed back the judgements to pupils. Writing, more clearly than any other language form illustrates to the teacher what the pupil has, or has not understood, and in British education at least it is the written expression of learning and understanding which retains the highest status as evidence of attainment and achievement in examinations. But what are the purposes of pupil writing in history? Actually, this question is a contraction of two linked questions: what do pupils write for and who do they write for?

Many of the ways in which we think about writing in schools derive from the work of the Schools Council 'Writing Across the Curriculum Project' in the 1970s. The project team drew distinctions between different modes of pupil writing and urged teachers to think clearly about the purposes and audience of pupil writing (see Figure 8.1). In the later 1980s, the National

Figure 8.1 Thinking about pupil writing. (From Martin, *et al.*, 1976.)

Transactional writing
Writing for presenting the 'facts' for reporting, arguing, persuading, convincing, analysing: the writer needs to consider the organization of ideas, logicality and truthfulness of publicly agreed knowledge.

Expressive writing
Reflecting the flow of the writer's thought processes and feelings: emotional and personal content is more important than the structure of the piece or its congruence with public knowledge. Diaries, personal letters and mediations provide opportunities for expressive writing.

Poetic writing
The language of fiction and poetry, where form and content are intertwined. Whilst there are imaginative elements in *transactional* and *expressive writing*, it is in poetic writing that imagination is at a premium. Poetic writing engages feelings and emotions.

Audience
Audiences for pupil writing might include:
● the writer
● a trusted adult
● a teacher as partner in dialogue
● the teacher as examiner
● a peer group
● some defined section of the public
● the public at large.

Writing Project tried to identify classroom strategies which would enhance the role of writing in pupil learning. The emphasis was on the nature of writing as a process rather than a series of products, a process involving preparation, drafting, revising and publishing. As a result of developments like these, the dominant tendency in the teaching of writing is now to encourage pupils to write 'real' texts for 'real' purposes and audiences, to clarify the distinctions between the generation of ideas and the drafting, redrafting and polishing of a finished text, and to encourage the production of more subjective or expressive written work.[1]

Since the 1970s, history teachers have tended to explain their classroom practice by reference to developing in pupils the 'skills' of the historian. By this they mean involving pupils during history lessons in activities which in one sense or another 'model' the activities of the historian: collecting, processing, analysing and synthesizing information relevant to a given topic or investigation. Although recent commentators, from a number of perspectives, have cast doubt on the validity of such 'modelling', we should begin by noting that even in those classrooms where there is considerable emphasis on the development of 'skills', relatively little explicit attention has been given to considering the place of pupil writing. This is not because writing does not go on in these classrooms, but perhaps because history teachers have generally shown remarkably little curiosity about the sorts of writing which pupils do, the ways in which different sorts of writing serve different purposes in both pupil learning and the understanding of history and the range of different registers and genres which are available to pupils and teachers. History teachers have, instead, relied on a single form of writing – *transactional report writing* in order to convey, often in relatively short amounts, *information* which has been gleaned from a resource: a textbook, a written primary source, a video or the teacher. Peter John's study of classroom history tasks in five schools suggested that the predominant modes of classroom writing in history for pupils are the production of reports and descriptive comprehension:

> 18 per cent of tasks were of the simple comprehension type. Descriptive questions accounted for 10 per cent, explanatory tasks made up 15 per cent while those asking for a report amounted to 16 per cent. . . . Very few opportunities were afforded to the pupil to engage in higher order thinking and writing which involved the skills of analysis, argument, persuasion and comparison.[2]

Writing in historical enquiry

If writing has a central place in classrooms, it plays an equally central role in the construction of academic history. We have relatively few accounts of the ways in which historians work, in the archives, in the library, in their study or in the seminar room, as opposed to the many accounts of the ways in which they think about the nature of their discipline. However, it can be suggested that historians, substantially, write for three different purposes in conducting a historical enquiry.

All historical work begins with the notion of enquiry: establishing what can be learnt about what happened, working it into an arguable interpretation, exploring and refining the interpretation in response to a specific question about the past. Historians write in order to note or *record* their reactions to ideas or to new material, they write in order to *organize* their material around the ideas which most appear to them to make sense of it and they write in order to *present* their ideas about that material. In the first case, the note is a part of the means by which the historian opens and sustains a dialogue with the raw materials of history: with the materials in the archive, with the findings and arguments of other historians. The note is part of the process of building an interpretation of the materials which exist for accessing the past. At this stage according to Barzun and Graff:

> a note is a first thought: . . . [ask yourself] am I simply
> doing clerk's work or am I assimilating new knowledge
> and putting down my own thoughts?

Note-making is an essential discipline of the historian: the collection of information, observations, the extraction of relevant material, the establishment of the structure of ideas. This is more than, for example, the stacking of photocopies or the transcription of information: it involves, suggests Pocock 'getting the structure [of the material] . . . into my bones'.[3] But information, material, ideas are not simply accumulated, they are collected in response to an enquiry, in response to a question about the past upon which data can be amassed. The process of acquiring information is, then, active: it is part of the process by which thinking about this question begins and proceeds. The data collected, from the archive, from other research, from textbook surveys and monographs will suggest other avenues for investigation and may show some initial questions to be fruitless. This is true of the way in which material is selected, but it is equally true of the way in which material is recorded, assimilated and organized. This idea of a series of 'dialogues' with the raw material of their work appears to be a defining characteristic of the way academic historians work. Wineburg's comparison of the ways in which academic historians conducted a historial enquiry with the ways in which school pupils conducted a similar enquiry, has already been quoted:[4]

The notion of an almost literal sense of dialogue at the core of historical enquiry leads us into the second central purpose of writing for historians: to organize raw materials around the focus of enquiry. Tosh points out that:

> Many historians who have a flair for working on primary sources find the process of composition excruciatingly laborious and frustrating. The temptation is to continue amassing material so that the time of reckoning can be put off indefinitely.

Writing here is more clearly a version of thinking around the material: drafts and sketches are begun, half-finished, rejected. Patterns are established; new material added and the patterns revised. Work here is provisional and personal: drafts are sketched and subsequently rejected, although the process of drafting such rejected patterns informs the eventual product. Thinking at this stage will involve diagrams, pencil sketches, lists, headings, gaps and question marks. Macaulay's struggles to shape his *History of England* show just how truculent the material can be (Figure 8.2). Pocock's account of the drafting and redrafting process in the construction of historical accounts suggests that 'the task of learning to think draws very close to the task of learning to write'.[5]

Finally, writing is undertaken to *report* the trains of thought and ideas to the wider community – to write history. G.R. Elton described 'the agony of forcing thought into order and pattern', deploying description, narrative and analysis in ways appropriate to the enquiry. Macaulay's difficulties in organizing the materials for his history are only the best documented account of the difficulties which all historians confront in shaping their materials. For academic historians, this *reporting* of conclusions, of what has been discovered and the attribution to it of structure and meaning is *always* a culmination of the process which began with the collection of material in response to a question or an enquiry, proceeded through the organization of material and led to the production of an account. The writing of a paper, a monograph or a text is always a way of bringing the enquiry to a culmination, or presenting albeit conclusions in relation to the question which was posed at the beginning of the process. This too is far from a final product:

Figure 8.2   Macaulay: the problems of organizing the *History of England*. (From Trevelyan, 1876.)

I have thought a great deal during the last few days about my History. The great thing about a work of this kind is the beginning. How is it to be joined to the preceding events? Where am I to commence it? . . . after much consideration I think that I can manage by the help of an introductory chapter or two, to glide imperceptibly into the full current of my narrative.

18 December 1838

Mere chronological order is not the order for a complicated narrative.

4 December 1848

To make the narrative flow as it ought, every part naturally springing from that which precedes; to carry the reader backward and forward across St George's Channel without distracting his attention, is not easy. Yet it may be done. I believe that this art of transitions is as important or nearly so, to history as the art of narration.

15 April 1850

Chapter XIV will require a good deal of work. I toiled on it some hours and now and then felt dispirited. but we must be resolute and work doggedly, as Johnson said. . . . Arrangement and transition are arts which I value much but which I do not flatter myself that I have attained.

1 January 1854

I worked hard at altering the arrangement of the first three chapters of the third volume. What labour it is to make a tolerable book and how little readers know how much trouble the ordering of the parts has cost the writer!

6 February 1854

. . . publication should not be delayed until all the results are in. To delay is only human; who wants to stand in error? And yet it is a bad policy for the time lag delays progress in our field as a whole and increases the possibility that in the end nothing at all will be published.[6]

Three clear ideas emerge from this process. In the first place, writing has a central place in the process of historical enquiry; it is never for its own sake, but generally to fulfil the wider purpose of collecting, organizing, or presenting understandings. Secondly, writing serves distinct purposes at different stages of the historical process: the purpose of the note, the sketched, subsequently rejected and then refined plan and the final report are all quite different. Thirdly, however, whilst writing serves a range of functions, it is always in some respect a *progress report*, always provisional and always part of a series of interlocking dialogues within the academic community, between the ideas and hunches historians have and the evidences they have uncovered. At some stages the progress report is a private one, at others, relatively public, but the *purpose* of writing is, viewed in terms of the process above, always akin to the purpose of a log.

Writing history in school

Does the process outlined above have parallels in the way history relates to language and ideas in the classroom? If we can understand the purposes of writing in the construction of understandings of the past, then it may help us to look again at the way pupils are generally asked to write in classrooms and to think about specifying the purposes of their writing with more care. Repeatedly, teachers bemoan some common traits in their pupils' writing: their answers are too short; they rely too heavily on other people's thoughts by copying out text from secondary accounts, or less defensibly, first-hand reports; their extended writing in history is less expansive, less profound and less *thoughtful* than their extended writing in, particularly English.[7] But if we consider the *purposes* of types of writing and their relationship to the construction of historical understandings we may help pupils to understand the place of writing in their learning rather more clearly.

Gathering information

Obviously, pupils need to acquire information about the past: they need to be able to move around in the publicly agreed territory of history, to realize the boundaries within which their own constructions of the past are set. The standard source for this information about the past has always been the teacher: as a pupil myself in a 1970's grammar school I wrote at dictation or from the chalkboard. As a variant, we laboriously copied text from weighty textbooks, and, as a relief, copied maps or diagrams. Perhaps for these reasons, teachers have felt reluctance about the practice of note-taking and the collection of information, and have substituted other techniques for them in the accumulation of information. Most notably, in both classrooms and in more recent textbooks they have adopted worksheet methods in which pupils accumulate information in response to short, often comprehension-based questions. As a response to the techniques such methods replaced, these strategies have one important strength and an equal, perhaps greater, weakness. They recognize that if we want pupils to collect information they need to have a structure in which to locate it. However, worksheets, sequences of questions on the chalkboard or in textbooks can fracture a topic so that the overall picture, the overall enquiry is obscured. Writing is done to show that you are not getting into trouble, to fill the gap until the end of the lesson. Once done, it is forgotten; it is there to fill the exercise book, to show that you are conforming. The difficulty with writing of this sort is not that it is about the accumulation of information, but that it does not present the writing task in its context as part of the process of building up interpretive understandings of the past.

If one of our concerns is to enhance the quality of writing and to extend pupils' abilities to express their ideas in writing, then these procedural questions need to be seen for what they are: staging posts on the route to the construction of historical understanding, or, to change the metaphor, scaffolding which will support the subsequent construction. These metaphors are significant: pupils need opportunities to build their thinking on secure scaffolding. Historians work in a not dissimilar way. Their field notes, archive notes or journals are scaffolding for the historical writing they will eventually do. The 'scaffolding' is vital to research, but significant only insofar as it relates to an overall enquiry through which new interpretive understanding is developed.[8]

History teachers are extremely effective at designing written work which allows pupils to accumulate information and which require them to make short-term judgements about what to write down, but they need to see such work for what it is: a strategy for data capture, for logging information which may be significant later and for noting initial reactions to information. That information may be used in a later piece of work, but equally it may be rejected; it may be useless for the enquiry being undertaken, but the judgement that it is useless is itself part of the enquiry process. If we ask pupils to 'Open the textbook at page 25 and complete the questions at the end', we can hardly argue that we are involving them in the exploration of historical ideas. Although the task may play a part in the construction of new knowledge, much of potential is being lost: we need to devise activities which ask them to make judgements about what they might expect to quarry from this book as opposed to another, to locate information, and to capture information, in a variety of forms, for future use. So an important, and neglected role for writing in the history classroom is precisely to capture data which will be used later. Part, then, of the job of the history teacher is to encourage pupils to experiment with different strategies for noting and reacting to new information and ideas.

Shaping ideas

Writing has a second, very seriously neglected second function in the classroom construction of historical understanding, which lies between the capture of data and its presentation as considered output. The stage of the writing process devoted to drafting and to revising is of critical importance in both shaping understanding and in refining the quality of the final product. Pupils in the 1990s with access to powerful wordprocessing and text editing and handling packages are fortunate, in ways that their predecessors were not: the potential exists to ensure that redrafting and revising is central to the production of written responses in history. Of course, text editing alone does not guarantee that revising will help pupils to focus on the quality of their ideas: pupils need to be encouraged to find patterns, to organize ideas, to find ways of expressing the information they have collected in ways which provide what Stephen Parker has called *conceptual plans* which are (Figure 8.3):

> based on language in its briefest form . . . powerful in
> terms of density of information and speed of use . . . to
> create an overall shape for the intended writing.[9]

Figure 8.3   Conceptual plans. (Based on Parker, 1993.)

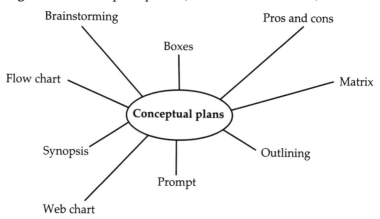

Conceptual plans can help to organize material around the enquiry or historical question. They can provide a shape which helps to make sense of the material, to look for patterns, to establish ways of thinking. They can help to identify gaps in information which can be supplemented through collecting more data. Conceptual plans can be individual or collaborative, and will generate new ways of looking at, and thinking about, the original problem. They will provide diagrammatic, illustrative ways of looking at the past: relationships will be indicated by arrows on charts as much as by conjunctions in sentences. This book was written at a wordprocessor: sections were drafted, revised and pasted to different parts of the text. But there were many occasions when planning took place using a sheet of A3 paper and a pencil. Ideas were sketched using diagrams and an eraser to rub out ideas which led nowhere. Thinking in this way helped me to construct the text.

Different types of history in the classroom – different historical questions – will suggest different sorts of approach to encouraging pupils to sketch their ideas. If we want pupils to analyse the short-, medium- and long-term causes of the French Revolution, we will want them to think in terms of diagrams and flow charts which emphasize relationships and pattern. If we want pupils to consider the sorts of attitudes, values and beliefs which led seventeenth century Puritans to set sail to America we will want them to explore different types of patterns. This stage of work –

which will involve sketching and drafting ideas – is precisely where Pocock's observation about the relationship between learning to write and learning to think connects with classroom history. We can overlook the need for pupils to explore historical ideas in this sort of way, to explore ideas through what Jerome Bruner has called the 'iconic' mode of representation, and yet it seems for pupils to be a particularly powerful way of expressing new understandings and exploring complex connections.

Producing accounts

Both the idea of using writing for data capture and the idea of writing to organize ideas are largely personal, although they might clearly emerge from and give support to collaborative classroom strategies: pupils need feedback on their strategies and they need support in developing effective strategies for collecting and organizing ideas, However, history is constructed – ideas about the past are organized – when we draw ideas about the past together. The construction of an historical account – an explanation, a description or a narrative of the problem which has been explored – is an important element of classroom history just as in historical enquiry outside schools. If we are asking historical questions of pupils, we have to allow them to learn to offer historical answers. Teachers have, quite rightly, pointed to the difficulties of such a task. They have suggested that many pupils find considerable difficulty in producing extended writing. They have realized, alongside researchers of the last thirty years, that many pupils condense their ideas when they are asked to commit them to paper, leaving too many points implicit. They have objected to the apparent attempt to make pupils leap through so many 'academic' hoops. And yet without this element of historical reconstruction, historical knowledge is incomplete: without the attempt to organize and present ideas to others, the past remains disconnected in the learner's mind.

The organization of extended writing is, for many pupils, very difficult, but there are important indications which suggest that the effort of developing their capacities to organize historical material is worthwhile. In the writing model explored here, the presentation of ideas is one stage in a process. It is suggested that a central task for us as teachers in supporting the development of historical understanding is the provision of written tasks as culminations of historical enquiries which extend pupils' capacity to think historically. This does not mean that they need be 'long' – whatever we might mean by that – but it does mean that they should be challenging in the ways they ask pupils to complete the move from the accumulation of material through the sketching of relationships to the presentation of a statement about the historical material which they have explored. In spite of the work of the Schools' Council in the 1970s, and in spite of the work of the National Writing Project in the 1980s, it remains the case that extended writing is relatively rare in the history classroom, and that when it is done it is written in the same exercise books as the procedural notes which precede it and for the same audience – the class teacher – as all other written work. It lacks both a clear sense of *audience* and a clear sense of *purpose*. Where the assumed audience for a piece of written work remains the teacher, imaginative classroom teachers are able to devise a variety of tasks which make themselves an accessible, somewhat disguised audience. There are, of course, many occasions when the teacher *is* the most appropriate audience for pupils' work, but it is also possible to produce work for other real or imagined audiences. Real audiences might include other pupils, in the same class or in other classes in the same school or even in other schools – for example, feeder primary schools. Adults outside the school, for example parents who might visit on a parents' evening, or older people in a community or day-care centre, or school governors are other possible audiences: pupils could produce wall displays, information leaflets, guide books, fact sheets and so on. But there are also imaginary audiences, contemporary or historical, and by the way in which we manipulate the expectations, we can vary the demands which the work places on pupils[10]:

- 'Produce a briefing report for the Board of Directors of a property company on archaeological remains and significance of a developer's site.'
- 'Here are two responses from last year's class. Was there a mistake in Amajit's answer? Was Sukhinder's better or worse?'
- 'Produce a magazine for children in the 1630s, or the 1830s.'
- 'Decide which five items from the 1580s, 1680s or whenever you would choose to put in a time capsule to be opened in a thousand years time, and explain to people in the year 2580 or 2680 what the items were used for.'
- 'Produce a guidebook to a local historic site for wheelchair

users, for very young children, or very old people, or American tourists.'

- 'Explain for a group of primary school children what you think the machinery shown in the diagram was for, and draw a sequence of diagrams to show how it worked. What was it designed for?'
- 'Produce an encyclopaedia entry of a set number of words explaining this subject for [choose audience].'
- 'Work in threes. Each of you is to write an obituary for King Henry VIII, one of them to be published just after his death in 1547, another after the accession of Queen Mary in 1553 and another after the accession of Queen Elizabeth in 1558.'

These are more than simply gimmicks, because the key point is to ask pupils to consider their audience as part of their work, so that they will need to think about how to lay ideas out, how to communicate connections, and how to choose appropriate language and linguistic forms to convey their understandings *in addition to the need to focus on historical concepts*. Of course, different pupils or groups of pupils in the class can produce items for different audiences and the results compared as part of the culmination of the activity. Different forms, different tasks, may release pupils from some of the constraints of form and style which other forms impose: if we ask pupils to construct a newspaper article, we imply different expectations of the product compared, say, to a government report. Nick Levine's analysis of the diary accounts produced by 15-year-old pupils makes the point well (Figure 8.4):

> the form of the writing released the students from
> constraints that would have made it hard for them to tackle
> more formal, impersonal kinds of writing. The diary form
> offered the student writers the chance to heighten their
> own natural language by imagining themselves inside the
> head of another person in another time. It might be argued
> that what is written will lack the discipline of orthodox
> history-writing; if that means that the pupils' writing will
> be unlike the teacher's, or the textbook writer's . . . then so
> be it for it is so.[11]

If audience and purpose provide linked opportunities to think about the sorts of writing which pupils might undertake in the classroom, they also provide opportunities to focus rather more

Figure 8.4   Pupils' diary accounts. (From Levine, 1981, p. 62.)

It was raining all day today – altogether boring. Liza Entwhistle the young mother who lives across the road from me was found dead early this morning. We all have reason to believe that she had diarrhoea and that she must have been in great pain before her death, she was also perspiring an awful lot. Her husband died of the same illness four days past. God only knows what will happen to her poor children.

Christina

Today across the yard we had news that one of the people had just got cholera. The smell was terrible, rats were the only things that went in and out of the houses. They dumped more and more rubbish in the yard by the pump. Again today I took the long walk to the pump at the other side of town. We felt that it was too late to move because I myself do not feel too well so I think this might be the last time I will write in my diary so signing off.

Kevin

carefully on the *range* of written work for audiences which might be considered. The range is enormous, and Stephen Parker's 'writing generator' is as good an *aide-mémoire* as any to the range of different genres from which pupils could be encouraged to select for experiment over the course of a school year. What is appropriate in some settings, for some purposes of interpretation will be less appropriate for others: sensitive teaching will enable appropriate possibilities to be negotiated (Figure 8.5).

This chapter has attempted to provide a thorough rationale in terms of the intellectual demands of classroom history for the types of written work which we might ask pupils to generate in classrooms. Also we have tried to distinguish between the *collection* of information, data and impressions, the *organization* of the material around historical questions and issues and the *presentation* of historical ideas. What follows from this is that we need both to be more explicit about the sorts of writing we ask pupils to undertake in classrooms and to be more rigorous about the ways in which we relate writing tasks to the underpinning purposes of teaching and learning history, in other words to the ways in which we ask pupils to construct their interpretations of

Figure 8.5 Types of writing: the writing generator. (From Parker, 1993, pp. 192–3.)

acknowledgement	gloss	poster
advertisement	graffiti	prayer
affidavit	greetings card	précis
announcement	guide	proclamation
article	headline	prospectus
autobiography	horoscope	questionnaire
ballad	instruction	recipe
biography	invitation	record
blurb	journal	reference
brief [legal]	label	report
broadsheet	letter (various types)	résumé
brochure	libel	review
caption	list	rule
cartoon	log	schedule
catalogue	lyric	script
certificate	magazine	sermon
charter	manifesto	sketch
confession	manual	slogan
constitution	memo	song
critique	menu	sonnet
crossword	minutes	specification (job)
curriculum	monologue	spell
curriculum vitae	news	statement
definition	notes	story
dialogue	notice	summary
diary	novel	syllabus
directory	obituary	synopsis
edict	pamphlet	telex
editorial	paraphrase	testimonial
epitaph	parody	travelogue
essay	petition	voice bubble
eulogy	placard	weather forecast
feature	play	will
forecast	poem	
form	postcard	

the past. Because understanding, and constructing knowledge about the past is extremely difficult, and because writing is a central way of clarifying ideas about the past, we have to employ writing with some degree of precision as a tool in supporting pupils' increasing confidence in handling ideas about the past. At root, we need to expect pupils to be able to explain confidently *why* they have written something down.

If the sort of process described for the generation of historical understanding in the classroom is accepted, then it also follows that we might expect pupils to undertake different sorts of writing at different stages of their historical enquiries in the classroom: the sorts of writing which are appropriate to the taking of notes, or to the organization of material are quite different from the sorts of writing which we will ask them to employ in the presentation of historical writing. The distinctions are familiar enough to the historian, and probably to the teacher; they are the distinctions between exploratory, tentative and personal purposes and considered, thought out, public purposes. One of the most powerful applications of information technology in the history classroom is to support this developmental approach to writing: providing opportunities to log ideas, to sketch out plans, to work the plans up to an interim and then a finished form without the time-consuming labour of rewriting, copying, and so on.

In the late 1980s, considerable work was done on the development of writing and writing policies in schools in Australia, and particularly by the New South Wales (NSW) Department of Education. This work focused both on the processes engaged in during the act of composing writing and on the completed product. Writing in order to gather, consider and re-order subject content, and the adaptation of different writing purposes to different stages of the writing process underpinned the extensive work on writing policy. What interests me here is the attempt to relate different forms of writing to different intellectual activities. Figure 8.6 adapts the model used by the NSW Education Department to stimulate teacher thinking about the place of writing in investigational work to the model of writing in history set out here.

The sort of thinking about writing which underpins this chapter depends on pupils having confidence in the way teachers will respond to their work, as provisional statements of ideas. The way in which teachers respond to the pupils' writing is a powerful way of shaping the way pupils think about their own writing, and the time and energy which is devoted to the discussion of the purposes of different writing tasks, their

Figure 8.6   The process of writing and the process of history. (Adapted from NSW Department of Education, Australia, 1987.)

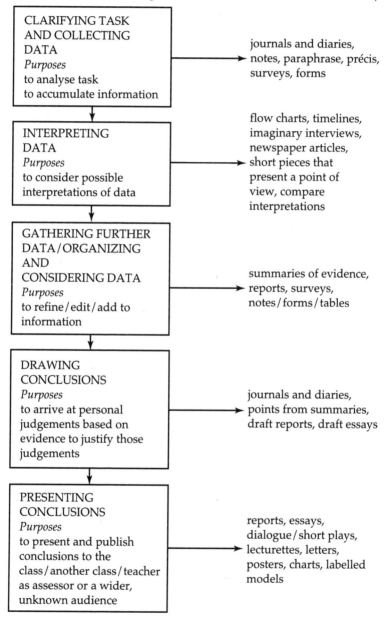

content, form and audience, and their place in learning is critical. At the heart of the issue is what Douglas Barnes and Yanina Sheeran have called the 'ground rules' of school writing:[12] the unspoken – and often unanalysed and indistinct – assumptions which underpin school writing tasks and which act as a powerful influence on the ways in which teachers and learners shape their reactions to what is asked and what is produced. Pupils need to grasp the purposes to which their writing will be put if they are to feel confident about the way they write. They need to understand clearly the sorts of judgement which will be made about their notes, their sketches and their finished products; for their part, too, teachers need to feel confident that it is appropriate to apply different sorts of judgement to different stages of the process of historical understanding, and this in turn demands a clarity about how different writing fits into that process.

None of the ideas used here undermine the central role of the teacher in supporting the way pupils undertake, revise and present writing, but they do provide us with a model which helps to relate different sorts of pupil writing to different stages in the generation of historical ideas. If writing, in all its forms is to serve pupils' attempts to sort out understandings, it requires, in addition, some pattern of dialogue between teacher and learner about what is written: pupils need opportunities to discuss the purpose of the writing, its possible forms and content and its intended audience. Teachers need, in the light of this, to think about what sort of comment, what sort of feedback and what sort of judgement it is appropriate to make. Equally, teachers need to feel confident that they have involved pupils in the making of judgements about their own work: prompting them to pose questions such as 'What have I found out from this work?', 'How well did I do?' and 'What stopped me doing better?'

Notes

1 On 'Writing Across the Curriculum Project', the work of the Schools Council Project is set out in N. Martin *et al.* (1976) *Writing and Learning Across the Curriculum 11–16*. London: Ward Lock. The work of the National Writing Project is best explored through SCDC (1989) *The National Writing Project 1: Writing and Learning*. London: SCDC. On collaboration and writing in the classroom, see especially M. Styles

(1989) *Collaboration and Writing*. Milton Keynes: Open University Press. On writing policy in schools, see Eve Bearne and Cath Farrow (1991) *Writing Policy in Action: the middle years*. Milton Keynes: Open University Press. Also B. Harrison (1994) *The Literate Imagination: renewing the secondary English curriculum*. London: David Fulton. See especially pp. 109–15. Harrison's central point is that writers 'need to give . . . attention to the discovery of *ideas*'. Considerable work on writing across the curriculum has been done in Australia; the oustanding guide is New South Wales Department of Education (1987) *Writing K-12*, and especially pp. 72–7 on the process of writing. I am grateful to Mike Hayhoe for this reference.

2 On classroom writing tasks in the humanities, see: P. John (1993) History tasks at Key Stage 3: a survey from five schools. *Teaching History*, 70: 18–19; P. John (1994) Academic tasks in history classrooms. *Research in Education*, 51: 11–22. As long ago as the Bullock Report, concern was expressed that much classroom 'writing' time was spent copying: see DES (1975) *A Language for Life*. London: HMSO. See also E. Spencer (1983) *Writing Matters Across the Curriculum*. London: Hodder and Stoughton. Douglas Barnes and Yanina Sheeran suggest that pupils laboriously copy anything down in the belief that some of it might be relevant. See Y. Sheeran and D. Barnes (1991) *School Writing: discovering the ground rules*, pp. 59–61. Milton Keynes: Open University Press. See also p. 68: 'copying . . . involved less effort . . . leaving the mind free to roam'.

3 On note-taking, see J. Barzun and H.F. Graff (1977) *The Modern Researcher*, 3rd edn, p. 23. New York: Harcourt Brace Jovanovitch. Also, J.G.A. Pocock (1970) Working on ideas in time in L.P. Curtis (ed.) *The Historian's Workshop*, p. 162. New York: Knopf.

4 On dialogues between researcher and sources, see S. Wineburg (1991) On the reading of historical texts: notes on the breach between School and Academy. *American Education Research Journal*, 28(3): 449–515; the quotation is from pp. 500, 503, see p. 93 above; also see Pocock, op. cit., p. 161: the historian 'may well end by basing his pattern on a quite limited number of sources, and if he knows how to do it properly he may do no more with those sources than sit and read, sit and think, sit and write'.

5 On the planning of historical accounts, see John Tosh (1984) *The Pursuit of History: aims, methods and new directions in the study of modern history*, pp. 93–106. London and New York: Longman. See also Pocock, op. cit., p. 161. See also Barzun and Graff, op. cit.

6 On writing, see G.R. Elton (1969) *The Practice of History*, p. 114. Glasgow: Collins Fontana. See also Tosh, op. cit., p. 106 and J. Vansina (1974) The power of systematic doubt in historical enquiry. *History in Africa*, 1(1): 111.

7 On writing in different subjects, see K. Perera (1984) *Children's*

Writing and Reading: analysing classroom language. Oxford: Blackwell, in association with Deutsch. The importance of personal involvement in writing for the quality of the product is discussed by Harrison, op. cit., pp. 162–8.

8 'Scaffolding': the metaphor is Bruner's, and is quoted in, and used in, K. Norman (ed.) (1992) *Thinking Voices: the work of the National Oracy Project*, p. 186. London: Hodder and Stoughton for the National Curriculum Council.

9 On pupil planning, see S. Parker (1993) *The Craft of Writing*, pp. 33–4. London: Paul Chapman Publishing. See also Barnes and Sheeran, op. cit, p. 120.

10 On types of writing in history: the ideas developed owe a great deal to my discussions with Martin Oldfield, Colin Shephard and others, as well as to the pioneering work of Chris Taylor and Gillian Temple. See especially Devon County Council (1994) *A Devon Approach to History at Key Stage 3*. Exeter: Devon County Council.

11 On extended writing in schools, see N. Levine (1981) *Language Teaching and Learning: History*, p. 63. London: Ward Lock. Levine's work on history teaching is exceptionally clear and thoughtful and also unjustifiably neglected in recent debates on the teaching of history. See also J. Moffett (1968) *Teaching the Universe of Discourse*. New York: Houghton Mifflin. Moffett observes that 'many underdeveloped high school students . . . write only synopses'.

12 Barnes and Sheeran, op. cit., p. 67, observe that 'writing summaries . . . of information contained in textbooks . . . limited children's ability to learn the constructional rules for themselves'.

Chapter 9

Making judgements

Teachers have always made judgements about pupils' work and learning. The judgements teachers make exert an enormous influence on learners. Making such judgements occupies a great deal of teacher activity: the way teachers think about how pupils respond to questions in classrooms, the impressions they pick up from listening to group discussions, the information they collect from pupils' written or diagrammatic work, the marks they award in more formal tests and examinations, the comments they write on reports for pupils and parents, the references they write for employers and higher education. All of these are occasions on which history teachers make judgements about their pupils' understandings of the past. They use various words to describe such occasions: observing, checking, marking, assessing, testing, examining, reporting, and so on; however, the underlying process of exercising judgement about the quality of pupil thinking is generally the same. Conventionally, we distinguish between two different purposes for these judgements:

- *Formative judgements* made by teachers to inform pupils about their learning, or by teachers to inform themselves about their pupils' learning. Formative judgements help teachers to plan future lessons and investigation, to provide work appropriate to pupils' understandings and attainments.
- *Summative judgements* made by teachers or others (examiners, for example) at the end of a unit or course. Summative judgements make a comment on what has already been achieved, and they may help to provide the basis for entry to further study or employment.

If there has been a shift in the balance of teachers' work in the last decade, it has been to emphasize the significance of summative assessment as a tool of accountability. In England and Wales, the introduction of the GCSE, the development of a centralized national curriculum, the increased emphasis on reporting progress to parents and the requirement on schools to publish their examination results have all entrenched the importance of apparently valid and reliable forms of assessment for teachers across the curriculum. Partly as a result, much routine, formative assessment has become more formal, its importance enhanced by the higher profile given to assessment generally. In response, teachers have experimented with a range of assessment techniques, involving group work, oral work, diagrammatic work and video-recordings in addition to more conventional written work. But all assessment, whatever its purpose or its form depends on the fundamental activity of making judgements. This chapter is concerned with the way we exercise those judgements in relation to pupils' understandings of the past, and in particular the way in which judgements can support the development of pupil thinking.

Some of the judgements we make as teachers are relatively straightforward ones: they are about whether pupils are accurately applying dating conventions, or whether they have correctly identified historical actors. These sorts of judgement are about whether pupils have acquired necessary information, and they are, of course, an essential element in learning about the past. However, very little of the work pupils routinely produce in the course of learning history is susceptible to this sort of correction. In most cases, we combine these judgements with others about the quality of pupils' ideas or writing. Where learning about the past is seen as a process of developing understandings as well as acquiring information, we need to consider the ways in which pupils develop and deploy understandings of historical processes, concepts and language. The exercise of judgement becomes more complex. We are teaching them particular history content but we are also aware of the need to develop their confidence and competence as learners over the sequence of topics we teach them, and we are aware of the way in which we need to develop their wider competencies – as writers, as thinkers, as learners.

When we respond to pupils' oral contributions we will make

some encouraging judgement ('That's a good way of putting it') but we will also choose an appropriate way of encouraging the pupil to think further, more deeply, to consider the implications of what was said. When we eavesdrop on a group discussion we will mentally note suggestions about ways in which the group could develop its ideas further ('Could you have made more effective use of the source by the Trade Union leaders?'). When we receive a piece of written work, we may indeed make factual corrections, and make some sort of judgement about its quality in relation to some set of criteria which we will summarize with a mark ('7/10', 'B−'). But we will probably do much more: we will make suggestions about how the piece could be improved. These suggestions will relate to the overall purpose of the work: the styles of thinking about evidence which it was intended to encourage, the imaginative reconstructions which it was intended to promote, the particular concepts, skills or ideas which it addressed. We will offer other ideas the learner might take into account, we will make some pointers as to the way in which the writing, and the writer need to develop. All these derive from our judgement about the status of the writing the learner has presented to us: they go far beyond 'marking' or 'assessment'; fairly obviously, they are 'teaching' activities. The judgements we make in responding to what pupils in lessons – the talk, the sketches, the completed work – are as much a part of the way in which we teach them as the way in which we devise activities. Assessment is part of the interaction in the classroom which helps pupils to develop their ideas about the past; used sensitively, like other elements in this interaction, it can enhance the quality of pupils' learning.[1]

Assessment and pupils' understandings of the past

Before we can think clearly about making judgements on pupil work in history we have to clarify the nature of the understanding we are attempting to map and assess: in other words, to identify the kinds of learning which history requires. So far, we have outlined an interpretive model of what constitutes *historical* understanding and knowledge, and indicated some of the ways this can be developed. The sort of historical understanding outlined can be characterized in a number of ways, but essentially, it rests on a concern to understand the particularity of human situations in time and context-bound situations. This sort of understanding is not reliant on formal logic based on *deductive inference* or *inductive reasoning* from the particular. Instead:[2]

> it is a process of adductive reasoning in the simple sense of adducing answers to specific questions so that a satisfactory 'fit' is obtained. The answers may be general or particular as the questions require. History is, in short, a problem-solving discipline. A historian is someone (anyone) who asks an open-ended question about past events and answers it with selected facts arranged in the form of a paradigm.

In the past, as we have seen, there was considerable doubt about pupils' ability to engage in this sort of historical thinking because of their age and level of cognitive development. Recent researchers have generally been less sceptical, suggesting that the limits on children's ability to understand the past seem to be set not so much by cognitive factors as by issues such as the teaching context, the nature of the task, the use of problematic and challenging historical materials or the teaching styles and subject knowledge of the teacher. Much recent work has broken down beliefs in age-related development in historical under-standing through three main findings. In the first place, a number of researchers have demonstrated the capacity of younger and less able pupils to come to terms with the strange-ness and complexity of much of the past, providing that ample time is given for pupils to explore materials in their own way. In these circumstances, pupils are able to develop distinctive elements of historical thinking in making inferences from evi-dence, deploying historical ideas and constructing accounts of past experiences. A second characteristic of pupils' historical thinking is that it appears to be highly uneven, sliding easily from the exceptionally sophisticated to the crassly obtuse. It does not proceed sequentially from one 'level' of competence to a more sophisticated 'level', but varies depending on the nature of the historical task and context. This, incidentally, is a reminder that pupil 'performance' on a given historical task can always be manipulated. Thirdly, as a result, pupils need to be engaged in a wide variety of activities – especially oral work and role-playing (see Chapter 6) – with adequate time for debate, analysis and the exchange of ideas. It follows that pupils cannot be expected to demonstrate their conceptual understandings of the past instantaneously and will often only show their capacity for thinking historically in the ebbs and flows of classroom activities rather than in short bursts of writing. Given the variety and range of demands of historical thinking, effective classroom work depends on clarity in specifying the purposes and demands of any given historical task. This clarity about purposes, about the demands and function of classroom work, is one of the most important ways in which teachers' own grasp of the nature of school history supports the learning of individual pupils.[3]

Evidence and judgement

Assessment judgements arise, then, from the work teachers do with pupils in classrooms. This evidence is typically made up of three elements, gathered by a combination of classroom observation and marking activity:[4]

- what pupils do (the classroom process)
- what pupils produce (classroom products)
- what teachers record

Each of these elements supports the exercise of judgement in assessing pupils. The argument throughout this book has been for an interpretive approach to the process of constructing historical understanding in the classroom. We have tried to identify elements of that process and relate them to classroom practice. The processes of talking and writing have been explored in Chapters 7 and 8 and provide settings which frame the sorts of work pupils will be asked to do in their history lessons. They indicate a pedagogy which allows pupils to develop their historical understandings by exploring ideas about the past in a variety of settings. Classroom tasks provide opportunities to develop skills, ideas and understandings because of the opportunities they provide to revisiting ideas in different contexts, spiralling through a term, a year or a school career. The classroom processes of talking, planning, investigating, writing, role-playing, and so on are central to the sorts of learning which goes on; we cannot separate the judgements we make about 'attainment' from the way in which pupils work in our classroom (Figure 9.1).

Figure 9.1   Ways of learning: interrelated strategies. (Based on discussions with Nigel Coulthard.)

- listening or observing
- talking about things in a small group
- presenting information to others in the group
- carrying out an investigation planned by the teacher
- carrying out an investigation planned by the learner
- or researching in a variety of books
- close study of one book
- putting ideas together from a variety of sources
- putting ideas together in connected writing
- putting ideas together in diagrams, charts
- manipulating data on a computer

It is always tempting to place emphasis on the products of pupil work in history, and these products are important: constructing accounts of the past, in writing, in pictures, in drama, in role-play, is an essential culmination of the process of understanding an element of the past. The product of a classroom activity, however simple or sophisticated is typically planned with a clear *historical* purpose in mind, because of the ideas we want pupils to explore through doing it, and we will at some point want to consider how successful it has been in allowing pupils to explore those ideas. The product of an investigation, or a piece of group work, or a reflective comment on a classroom discussion is an important piece of pupil work which demands appropriate attention: the process is as important as the product, but it is not more important. However, such products are inevitably 'snapshots' of pupil understanding: Camilla has produced an excellent, detailed, thorough and meticulous account of the reasons for the execution of Louis XVI, but her work on the Fall of the Bastille was less assured, less confident and less effective. Both demand a response, sensitive to the way she worked, and the quality of what she produced. The response will provide Camilla with a comment on what she has achieved in relation to the overall target of each piece of work, and *usable* specific guidance on how she might develop the quality of her work. Neither, though, provides us with a definitive answer about

Figure 9.2 Some purposes of assessment in history (ILEA, 1983: 40–1).

For groups:
- Identifying aspects of learning with which the majority of learners are confident and need spend no more time on.
- Identifying particular ideas, concepts, skills which can be demonstrated at a variety of levels of sophistication to see if a number of pupils are 'clustering' around a particular level.
- Identifying areas of historical understanding which are difficult for most/all members of the group.

For individual pupils:
- Identifying areas of learning which the pupil has mastered.
- Identifying areas of learning which the pupil is ready to explore more deeply.
- Identifying areas of learning a pupil is finding difficult.
- Providing a basis for detailed dialogue with a pupil about his or her learning so that he or she can begin to see *how* to develop.

Camilla's 'attainment' in history: they are pieces of evidence which support a provisional judgement (Figure 9.2). *Because* pupils' historical understanding is variable from context to context, with both progression and regression, individual products or pieces of work will in themselves provide only snapshots of pupil ability and competence.

This is why the third source of evidence retains its importance. Marks in markbooks are the everyday currency of teacher judgement. In shorthand, but at their best very flexible forms, they provide material to support the formulation of teacher judgements about pupil achievement. They log a summary comment on the outcome of a piece of work, but far more important than this they provide a map of the conditions under which different pieces of work were done, of the resources – physical, support, time – which were available to the learners. The markbook reminds us of particularly effective, or informative work. Again, the judgement itself is not in the markbook, but the markbook triggers off the location of evidence which will support the development of our judgement. We may need to supplement the traditional, shorthand markbook with something else; not with the complex grids and checklists of objectives-dominated assessment schemes but with something else which logs evidence to support the making of judgement: perhaps a notebook, a page for each pupil, which we use for brief jottings about their work in progress, about insights and comments they make in the course of their historical work, which is not a formal assessment judgement but an observational jotting of what the pupil did on a particular date. The accidental technological development of the 'Post-it' slips produced a very helpful tool: notes can be made quickly in a busy classroom and later stuck into the observation handbook.

The making of assessment judgements can bring with it a barrage of 'technology' which is 'applied' to pupils: they are 'given' marks; they are 'set' tests; they are 'reported' on. But there is no reason why this should be so, and the model of historical learning which argued here suggests that it is of limited utility. Over the last fifteen years or so, considerable effort has been invested in developing strategies which involves pupils in assessing their own development, and the argument has generally been that these strategies help pupils understand what they are being asked to do so that they can work more effectively. In one survey of assessment approaches involving pupils,

> teachers who were involved in the work were virtually unanimous in seeing the benefits. . . . They thought that making pupils aware of their specific problems and their strengths made them more willing to seek help.[5]

For pupil involvement in assessment to become genuinely useful for teachers and pupils, two things appear to be necessary. The first is a genuine attempt on teachers' part to communicate to pupils what is involved in learning, what expectations teachers have of their achievements in particular tasks. The second, and probably more challenging for teachers in an overcrowded curriculum, is an attempt to create the time to give self-assessment credibility and a place in pupil–teacher dialogue. In practice, it need not be overly time-consuming: pupils who are encouraged to make a brief note at the end of a piece of written work about what they found difficult, or easy, about the task, or pupils who make an initial assessment of their own achievement against some clearly articulated criteria are already beginning to play a part in thinking about their own learning. Again, complex,

Figure 9.3   Core assessment questions.

- Are pupils aware of what they are learning?
- Are pupils aware of why they are learning it?
- Are pupils able to recognize their progress in learning?

objectives-dominated checksheets are more likely to fail than modest, frequent adaptations to classroom routine which allow teacher and pupils to focus on the core purposes of assessment (Figure 9.3).

Assessment is always a provisional judgement on what pupils have learned; it is always a response to their attempts to reconstruct a past circumstance or situation. It is always, there-fore, an element in a dialogue between different views, different perceptions of the past. The judgements we make are part of the dialogue we have about the past.

Notes

1 On the nature of assessment in school history, the clearest introduc-tion remains HMI (1985) *History in the Primary and Secondary Years*, pp. 20–2. London: HMSO. The ideas are developed clearly by C. Culpin (1994) Making progress in history in H. Bourdillon (ed.) *Teaching History*, pp. 125–52. London: Routledge, for the Open Uni-versity. The wider range of teacher comment on pupil (written) work is cogently explored in N. Levine (1981) *Language Teaching and Learning: History*, pp. 78–80. London: Ward Lock.

2 On adductive historical thinking, see D.H. Fischer (1971) *Historians' Fallacies: towards a logic of historical thought*, p. xv. London: Routledge and Kegan Paul. The idea is deployed in relation to pupils' thinking by M.B. Booth (1979) 'A longitudinal study of cognitive skills, concepts and attitudes of adolescents studying a modern world history syllabus and an analysis of their adductive historical thinking'. Unpublished PhD thesis, Reading University. The distinctive nature of historical explanations are discussed, from different but in many ways conver-ging perspectives by J.H. Hexter (1972) *The History Primer*, Chapter 1. London: Penguin. Also E.P. Thompson (1978) *The Poverty of Theory*. London: Merlin.

3 On the capacity of children to achieve historical understandings, see M.B. Booth (1980) A modern world history course and the thinking of

adolescent pupils. *Educational Review*, 32(3): 245–57. Also M.B. Booth (1983) Skills concepts and attitudes: the development of adolescent children's historical thinking. *History and Theory*, 22(4): 101–17, demonstrates the holistic nature of much pupil thinking. See also A.K. Dickinson and P.J. Lee (1984) Making sense of history in A.K. Dickinson, P.J. Lee and P.J. Rogers (eds) *Learning History*. London: Heinemann. H. Cooper (1995) *History in the Early Years*. London: Routledge, demonstrates younger pupils' capacity to achieve historical understanding. The significance of teacher knowledge *irrespective of teaching style* underpins S. Wineburg and S. Wilson (1991) Subject matter knowledge in the teaching of history. *Advances in Research in Teaching, Vol. 2*, pp. 305–47. Greenwich, Connecticut: JAI Press. The unevenness of historical thinking is identified in J. Fines and R. Verrier (1974) *The Drama of History*. London: New University Press, as well as in Wineburg op. cit. and Dickinson and Lee, op. cit.

4 On classroom approaches to assessment, see M.B. Booth and C. Husbands (1993) The history National Curriculum in England and Wales: assessment at Key Stage 3. *Curriculum Journal*, 4(1): 21–36, especially pp. 34–6. I am indebted to Jim Harrison for our numerous discussions of approaches to assessment.

5 On involving pupils in assessment, the quotation is taken from B. Dockrell (1995) Approaches to educational assessment in C. Desforges (ed.) *An Introduction to Teaching: psychological perspectives*, p. 320. Oxford: Blackwell. For examples of pupil involvement in assessment in history, see N. Levine, op. cit., pp. 78–80. Also ILEA (1983) Language and history in *History and Social Sciences at Secondary Level*, 2, p. 41. London: ILEA. A. Farmer and P. Knight (1994) *Active History in Key Stages 3 and 4*, pp. 125–6. London: David Fulton, discuss peer- and self-assessment in useful, if brief, terms.

Chapter 10

So, what *is* history teaching?

> **What is history teaching?**
>
> What is a History teacher? He's someone who teaches
> mistakes. While others say, 'Here's how to do it,' he says,
> 'And here's what goes wrong.' While others tell you, 'This
> is the way, this is the path,' he says, 'And here are a few
> bungles, botches, blunders and fiascoes . . . ' It doesn't
> work out; it's human to err. . . . He's an obstructive
> instructor, treacherous tutor. Maybe he's a bad influence.
> Maybe he's not good to have around.
>   Graham Swift (1987) *Waterland* London: Heinemann.

Throughout this book we have explored the ways in which pupils
might build up understandings of the past in classrooms. Some
parallels between school history and recent developments in the
wider philosophy and practice of history have been drawn on. In
this final chapter, some assumptions about this relationship will
be made more explicit and we will draw together the ideas
explored earlier in the book.

History, of course, has always been a controversial subject in
the school curriculum. When we teach history, we choose some
content and leave out other content; we choose textbooks with
some perspectives and we neglect others. In the Soviet Union in

the late 1980s, *glasnost* made it possible to compare official Soviet accounts with versions of the same events written in the West. As a result of the discrepancies, Mikhail Gorbachev cancelled national high school history examinations because, he said, there was no point in testing pupils' knowledge of lies. The history we choose to teach our pupils is always a reflection of the assumptions of the society in which we live.

Many of the debates in western societies about the teaching and learning of history in schools have also been debates about the nature of national 'culture' and 'civilization'.[1] They are debates about what counts as 'significant' knowledge about the past, about how we select some historical knowledge and some historical events for their significance to our, and to succeeding generations. In many pre-modern societies, the past was communicated by oral traditions which changed and adapted traditions to the needs and concerns of succeeding generations. The emergence, during the nineteenth century, of a 'scientific' model of history supplanted pre-modern conceptions of the relationship between the present and the past. Progressively, after the 1840s, the notion of a 'scientific' history emerged, with clear canons of historical procedure. The characteristic of the 'new' history of the mid- and late-nineteenth century was its concern with 'facts' above all else. In 1900, a French historian at the First International Congress of Historians urged his professional colleagues to concern themselves with:

> Facts, facts, facts – which carry within themselves their
> lesson and their philosophy. The truth, the whole truth
> and nothing less than the truth.[2]

This model of historical learning was influential in the universities in the late nineteenth and early twentieth centuries, but it was even more influential in the schools. In spite of the early work of M.W. Keatinge, who argued in the years before 1910 for the deployment of historical evidence in the teaching of history, there seems little doubt the history teaching for much of the twentieth century worked within the general model David Sylvester has characterized as the 'great tradition' in which:[3]

> The history teacher's role was didactically active; it was to
> give pupils the facts of historical knowledge and to ensure
> through repeated short tests that they had learned them.
> The pupil's role was passive; history was a 'received

subject'. The body of knowledge to be taught was also clearly defined. It was mainly political history, with some European, from Julius Caesar to 1914.

By the 1960s, the positivist model of historical knowledge which underpinned these conceptions of history and school history was crumbling. As early as the 1920s, Carl Becker and Charles Beard in America had developed a more relativist model of history in which 'everyman' would write his own history. On this version of the historical enterprise, history functioned less as an objective account of the past and more as a cultural myth. Facts were not discovered; instead, declared Beard, the historian worked by 'subjective decision, not a purely objective discovery'. Forty years later, the upsurge of interest in Marxism, in social history 'from below' and in cultural history developed the concept of the historian's task in unanticipated ways. Some historians aspired to write 'total' history by asking novel questions of untapped sources and broadening the scope of the historical discipline by deploying new techniques derived from the social sciences.[4]

In schools, in the 1960s, history appeared to be sliding into a state of what one commentator called 'danger'. In some schools history was being squeezed off the school timetable by courses in social studies or humanities; school-leavers repeatedly said that history courses were dull and did not equip them for life after school. In an increasingly multicultural society, the monocultural emphases of Sylvester's 'great tradition' appeared to an increasingly graduate history teaching force to be less defensible and to cut school history off from the invigorating developments they had encountered at university. It was against this background that the Schools Council History Project, set up in 1972, set out to redefine the nature of school history. In place of a justification for history organized solely around culture and content, the Project offered an explicitly constructivist model of learning history. Whilst history lacked the clear conceptual structure of mathematics or science, the Project nonetheless defined a curriculum rationale for school history based on organizing concepts and historical skills: pupils would learn history as historians did, by practising, or constructing it in the classroom. By the mid-1980s, the Project philosophy was probably dominant in English schools.[5]

From the perspective of the mid-1990s, the claims made for both developments in social history and constructivist approaches to school history now appear somewhat unsophisticated. Post-modern critiques of history have challenged many of the claims of the discipline. History has been described as an intellectual by-product of modernity, its claims to generate 'knowledge' by examining 'facts' unsustainable; the problems historians choose to examine, the sources they use to address them and the theories they deploy in answering these problems have all been seen as essentially subjective. We have already quoted Hayden White's view that historians characteristically deploy one of a limited number of narrative modes in writing their historical accounts; for White, 'historians do not build up knowledge that others might use but generate discourses about the past'. Descombes has gone further and asserted that 'History is the western myth'.[6]

At the same time, the constructivist model of school history has come under twin attacks. Some critics, influenced by the intellectual critique of post-modernism have argued that constructivist models of school history were always epistemologically naïve. The notion that pupils can 'model' the historian's task precisely ignores the social context under which historical knowledge is constructed: historians do not come to a set of historical sources with an empty or open mind, but deploying a series of hypotheses and questions derived from their acquaintance with the work of other historians. Under the circumstances of the classroom, it is naïve to believe that pupils can acquire access to provisional understandings of the historical past by working on historical sources, by using the historical imagination.

The second prong of attack comes from a strain of intellectual conservatism which wishes to restore the 'great tradition' of the early and mid-twentieth century. Like the post-modernists, conservative critics resist both the claims made for constructivist approaches to school history and many of the claims made for social history. For them, school history fulfils an essentially socializing and integrative role, introducing pupils to the intellectual and cultural traditions of the society of which they will become adult members.[7]

History is concerned with attempting to understand the past. The accumulation of knowledge and understanding about the past is a core preoccupation for history teachers. We want our pupils to be building up ideas, understandings and knowledge about the past. But these ideas and understandings, this knowledge is in practice far from straightforward. There *is* simply too much history for any pupil to learn or for any teacher to teach. Some selection has to be made. Once that is acknowledged, there have to be clear, and publicly agreed, criteria for selecting the history which is to be taught. The richness of the historical past is its complexity. There are kings and queens, battles and wars, heroes and villains, but also women and children, slavery and factories, work and play. History is, more than anything else, about the experiences of different people, often under quite appalling conditions of poverty, ignorance, disease and in-humanity. More than this, however, the post-modern critique of historical objectivity reminds us that one group's heroes are another group's villains: those who are freedom fighters to some are terrorists to others. Those who are condemned as terrorists in one generation may be lauded as popular heroes in the next. In a fractured, multicultural society it is neither realistic nor sustain-able to assume that the history of a spacious 'common culture' will restore the 'great tradition', but it is more imperative than ever to engage pupils in enquiries into, and dialogue about, the legacies of the past.

It will be clear by now that knowing about the past is never just about knowing 'when things happened'. If pupils cannot begin to explain why they happened, with what consequences and effects, if they cannot explain why some historical periods and events have a significance and resonance *for them* if, in short, they cannot develop an intepretive framework for their understandings of the past, then knowing about the past is reduced to a sort of quiz game. For this reason, understanding the past is inseparably also about finding out what evidence exists, how it might be interpreted, what limitations it has, and about how historical events might be described by different commentators. In a complex, changing society, it is naïve to expect that easy consensus will be achieved on the proper concerns of school history.

Does this abandon the territory of school history to post-modern doubts about the intellectual viability of the subject? It does seem unarguable that historical enquiry is inextricably bound up with the preoccupations of the present and that historical accounts are always constructed to satisfy the needs of the audience for whom they were intended. There is no arguable case for a single model of 'historical objectivity', or of 'historical truth'. Nonetheless, the past once existed. History is not simply an enterprise in fiction because it involves procedures of dialogue with evidence, with the voices, however imperfectly mediated, of the past. We, and our pupils, have to establish a relationship with the past and with the way in which we, and they, make sense of the experiences of other people in different settings:

> History fulfils a human need by reconstituting memory
> . . . the renewable source of energy behind these
> [historical] inquiries comes from an intense craving about
> what it is to be human.[8]

This means that we need to establish a more subtle, less absolutist[9] understanding of the way in which knowledge is created. Our knowledge of the world and the language with which we describe it is not simply in our own heads, nor is it a given feature of the world in which we are living. It needs to be developed through the process of enquiry in classrooms, by teachers and learners in classrooms working to create meanings. Historical enquiry is not to be cut off from personal experience, nor is it to be locked into personal experience. It is fundamentally a way of relating the internal, the personal to the external, the public:

> History . . . offers a variety of tools for effecting liberation
> from intrusive authority, outworn creeds and counsels of
> despair. Historical analysis teaches that members of
> society raise structures that confine people's actions and
> then build systems of thought that deny those structures.
> It also suggests that all bodies of knowledge acquire
> ideological overtones because their meaning is too potent
> to be ignored. . . . [It] point[s] to the power of a revitalised
> public, when operating in a pluralistic democracy with
> protected dissent to mediate intelligently between society
> and the individual, knowledge and passion, clarity and
> obfuscation, hope and doubt. Telling the truth takes a
> collective effort.[10]

The future

People are always shouting that they want to create a
better future. It's not true. The future is an apathetic void

of no interest to anyone. The past is full of eager life, there to irritate, provoke and insult us, tempt us to destroy it or repaint it. The only reason people want to be masters of the future is to change the past. They are fighting for access to the laboratories where photographs are retouched and biographies and history re-written.

> Milan Kundera (1982) *The Book of Laughter and Forgetting*.
> London: Faber & Faber.

Notes

1 On approaches to the teaching and learning of history, see Marc Ferro (1984) *The Use and Abuse of History: how the past is taught*. London: Routledge Kegan Paul. Ferro explores the ways in which history is used in schools in a variety of cultural settings. For a conservative perspective on school history, see Helen Kedourie (1987) *The Errors and Evils of the New History*. London: Centre for Policy Studies, and, more generally on the conservative critique of relativist approaches to culture and education, see A. Bloom (1987) *The Closing of the American Mind: how higher education has failed democracy and impoverished the souls of today's students*. New York: Simon and Schuster.

2 On 'scientific' models of history the quotation is drawn from P. Novick (1988) *That Noble Dream: the objectivity question and the American historical profession*, p. 38. Cambridge: Cambridge University Press. On the development of the concept of a historical profession, see the summary in P. Burke (1991a) Overture: the new history its past and its future in Peter Burke (ed.) *New Perspectives on Historical Writing*, pp. 1–23. Oxford: Polity Press.

3 On the traditions of twentieth century history teaching, see D. Sylvester (1994) Change and continuity in history teaching, 1900–1993 in H. Bourdillon (ed.) *Teaching History*, p. 9. London: Routledge, for the Open University and for a briefer account J. Slater (1989) *The Politics of History Teaching: a humanity dehumanized?*, p. 1. Special Professorial Lecture, London: Institute of Education. See also V. Chancellor (1970) *History for their Masters: history in the school textbook, 1800–1914*. London: Penguin.

4 On relativist models of history, Becker and Beard's work is set out in Novick, op. cit., pp. 27–9. For a fuller statement of the relativist case, see E.H. Carr (1961) *What is History?* London: Penguin.

5 On curriculum development in history in the 1960s and 1970s, see M. Price (1968) History in danger. *History*, 53: 342–7; also Schools Council

(1976) *A New Look at History*. Edinburgh: Holmes McDougall. An outline of the Project's aims and achievements is set out in Sylvester, op. cit.

6 On post-modern approaches to history, Descombes is quoted by J. Appleby, L. Hunt and M. Jacob (1994) *Telling the Truth about History*, p. 232. New York, London: Norton. See Chapter 6, 'Postmodernism and the crisis of modernity', more generally. White is quoted on p. 245. Parallel developments in the study of the 'classical' past and postmodern approaches to archaeology are explored in M. Shanks (1996) *Classical Archaeology of Greece: experiences of the discipline*, pp. 173–6, 178–9. London: Routledge.

7 On critiques of constructivist approaches to history teaching, the post-modern critique is set out in K. Jenkins (1991) *Rethinking History*. London: Routledge. The conservative critique is most clearly elaborated in Kedourie, op. cit., but also underpins R. Skidelsky (1988b) History as social engineering. *The Independent*, 1 March 1988.

8 J. Appleby, L. Hunt and M. Jacob, op. cit., pp. 267–8. See also J. Slater (1995) *Teaching History in the New Europe*, pp. 6–8 and 133–6. London: Cassell and Council of Europe. Slater insists (p. 136) 'history cannot purge us of our subjective reactions to the past. What it can do is to oblige us to face them and scrutinize them'.

9 On 'less absolutist' models of collaborative enquiry, I owe the word 'absolutist' and some of the arguments with which I conclude, to J. Appleby, L. Hunt and M. Jacob., op. cit., pp. 247, 258, 308–9.

10 J. Appleby, L. Hunt and M. Jacob, op. cit., pp. 308–9.

Bibliography

Adams, R. (1992) *Expansion Trade and Industry*. Ormskirk: Causeway Press.

Appleby, J., Hunt, L. and Jacob, M. (1994) *Telling the Truth about History*. New York, London: Norton.

Bage, G. (1995) Chaining the Beast: an examination of how the pedagogic use of spoken stories may make historical narrative richer and more susceptible to analysis by children. An autobiographical research study by an advisory teacher. Unpublished PhD thesis, University of East Anglia.

Bann, S. (1990) *The Inventions of History: essays on the representation of the past*. Manchester: Manchester University Press.

Barnes, D. (1976) *From Communication to Curriculum*. London: Penguin.

Barzun, J. and Graff, H.F. (1977) *The Modern Researcher*, 3rd edn. New York: Harcourt Brace Jovanovitch.

Baugh, A.C. and Cable, T. (1978) *A History of the English Language*, 3rd edn. London: Routledge Kegan Paul.

Bearne, E. and Farrow, C. (1991) *Writing Policy in Action: the middle years*. Milton Keynes: Open University Press.

Bevir, M. (1994) Objectivity in history. *History and Theory*, 34(3): 328–44.

Bloom, A. (1987) *The Closing of the American Mind: how higher education has failed democracy and impoverished the souls of today's students*. New York: Simon and Schuster.

Bloom, B.S. (1956) *A Taxonomy of Educational Objectives. I*. London: Longman.

Booth, M. (1979) A longitudinal study of cognitive skills, concepts and attitudes of adolescents studying a modern world history syllabus and an analysis of their adductive historical thinking. Unpublished PhD thesis, Reading University.

Booth, M. (1987) Ages and concepts: a critique of the Piagetian approach to history teaching in C. Portal (ed.) *The History Curriculum for Teachers*, pp. 22–38. Lewes: Falmer.

Booth, M.B. (1980) A modern world history course and the thinking of adolescent pupils. *Educational Review*, 32(3): 245–57.

Booth, M.B. (1983) Skills concepts and attitudes: the development of adolescent children's historical thinking. *History and Theory*, 22(4): 101–17.

Booth, M.B. (1993) *The Teaching and Learning of History: a British perspective*. Göteborgs Universitet: Projektet Europa och Läroboken.

Booth, M.B. and Husbands, C. (1993) The history National Curriculum in England and Wales: assessment at Key Stage 3. *Curriculum Journal*, 4(1): 21–36.

Brooks, R., Aris M. and Perry, I. (1994) *The Effective Teaching of History*. Harlow: Longman.

Bruner, J. (1986) *Actual Minds, Possible Worlds*. Harvard: Harvard University Press.

Burke, P. (1991a) Overture: the new history its past and its future in P. Burke (ed.) (1991) *New Perspectives on Historical Writing*, pp. 1–23. Oxford: Polity Press.

Burke, P. (1991b) The history of events and the revival of narrative in P. Burke (ed.) *New Perspectives on Historical Writing*, pp. 233–47. Oxford: Polity Press.

Burke, P. (1992) *History and Social Theory*. Oxford: Polity Press.

Butterfield, H. (1924) *The Historical Novel: an essay*. Cambridge: Cambridge University Press.

Carr, E.H. (1961) *What is History?* London: Penguin.

Chancellor, V. (1970) *History for their Masters: history in the school textbook, 1800–1914*. London: Penguin.

Claxton, G. (1993) Minitheories: a preliminary model for learning science in P.J. Black and A.M. Lucas (eds) *Children's Informal Ideas in Science*. London: Routledge.

Collingwood, R.G. (1939) *An Autobiography*. Oxford: Oxford University Press.

Coltham, J.B. and Fines, J. (1970) *Educational Objectives for the Study of History*. London: Historical Association.

Cooper, H. (1992) *The Teaching of History*. London: David Fulton.

Cooper, H. (1995) *History in the Early Years*. London: Routledge.

Corfield, P. (1991) *Language, History and Class*. Oxford: Blackwell.

Culpin, C. (1994) Making progress in history in H. Bourdillon (ed) *Teaching History*. London: Routledge, for the Open University.

Darnton, R. (1984) *The Great Cat Massacre and Other Episodes in French Cultural History*. New York: Basic Books.

Davies, N.Z. (1973) *The Return of Martin Guerre*. Cambridge, Massachusetts: Harvard University Press.

Davies, N.Z. (1987) *Fiction in the Archives*. Oxford: Polity Press.

Davies, N.Z. (1988) On the lame. *American Historical Review*, 93(3): 575–8.

DES (1975) *A Language for Life*. London: HMSO.

Dickinson A.K. and Lee, P.J. (1978) Understanding and research in A.K. Dickinson and P.J. Lee (eds) *History Teaching and Historical Understanding*, pp. 94–120. London: Heinemann.

Dickinson, A.K. and Lee P.J. (1984) Making sense of history in A.K. Dickinson, P.J. Lee and P.J. Rogers (eds) (1984) *Learning History*. London: Heinemann.

Dickinson, A.K., Gard, A. and Lee, P.J. (1978) Evidence in history and the classroom in A.K. Dickinson and P.J. Lee (eds) *History Teaching and Historical Understanding*, pp. 1–17. London: Heinemann.

Dockrell, B. (1995) Approaches to educational assessment in C. Desforges (ed.) *An Introduction to Teaching: Psychological Perspectives*, pp. 307–24. Oxford: Blackwell.

Dorwald, D.C. (1974) Ethnography and administration: the study of Anglo-Tiv 'working misunderstanding'. *Journal of African History*, 15(3): 457–77.

Edwards, A.D. (1978) The 'language of history' and the communication of historical knowledge in A.K. Dickinson and P.J. Lee (eds) *History Teaching and Historical Understanding*, pp. 54–71. London: Heinemann.

Edwards, D. and Mercer, N. (1992) *Common Knowledge*. London: Routledge.

Elton, G.R. (1969) *The Practice of History*. Glasgow: Collins Fontana.

Elton, G.R. (1970) What sort of history should we teach? in M. Ballard (ed.) *New Movements in the Study and Teaching of History*. London: Temple Smith.

Farmer A. and Knight, P. (1994) *Active History in Key Stages 3 and 4*. London: David Fulton.

Ferro, M. (1984) *The Use and Abuse of History: how the past is taught*. London: Routledge Kegan Paul.

Fines, J. (1994) Evidence: the basis of the discipline? in H. Bourdillon (ed.) *Teaching History*, pp. 36, 122–6. London: Routledge.

Fines, J. and Verrier, R. (1974) *The Drama of History*. London: New University Press.

Finlay, R. (1988) The refashioning of Martin Guerre. *American Historical Review*, 93(3): 553–74.

Fischer, D.H. (1971) *Historians' Fallacies: towards a logic of historical thought*. London: Routledge and Kegan Paul.

Gard, A. and Lee, P.J. (1978) 'Educational objectives for the study of history' reconsidered in A.K. Dickinson and P.J. Lee (eds) *History Teaching and Historical Understanding*. London: Heinemann.

Gardiner, H. (1992) Surprisingly disciplined squads in K. Norman (ed.)

Thinking Voices: the work of the National Oracy Project, pp. 196–202. London: Hodder and Stoughton, for the National Curriculum Council.

Geertz, C. (1972) *The Interpretation of Cultures*. London: Hutchinson.

Giles P. and Neal, G. (1983) History teaching analysed in J. Fines (ed.) *Teaching History*, pp. 170–3. London: Holmes MacDougall.

Gill, D. (1987) History textbooks: education or propaganda. *Multicultural Teaching*, 7(2): 31–5.

Ginzburg, C. (1980) *The Cheese and the Worms: the cosmos of a sixteenth-century miller*. Baltimore: Johns Hopkins Press.

Gould, S.J. (1990) *Wonderful Life: the Burgess Shale and the Nature of History*. New York: Hutchinson.

Gunning, D. (1978) *The Teaching of History*. London: Croom Helm.

Harnett, P. (1993) Identifying progression in children's understanding: the use of visual materials to assess primary school children's learning in history. *Cambridge Journal of Education*, 23(2): 137–54.

Harrison, B. (1994) *The Literate Imagination: renewing the secondary English curriculum*. London: David Fulton.

Hexter, J.H. (1972) *The History Primer*. London: Penguin.

HMI (1985) *History in the Primary and Secondary Years*. London: HMSO.

Hooper-Greenhill, E. (1991) A new communication model for museums in G. Kavanagh (ed.) *Museum Languages: objects and texts*, pp. 49–63. Leicester: Leicester University Press.

Howe, A. (1992) *Making Talk Work*. London: Hodder and Stoughton.

Husbands, C. (1992a) Objects and interpretations in museum education. *Journal of Education in Museums*, 13: 1–4.

Husbands, C. (1992b) Facing the facts: history in schools and the curriculum in P. Black (ed.) *Education: Putting the Record Straight*. Stafford: Network Educational Press.

Husbands, C. and Pendry, A. (1992) *Whose History? School History and the National Curriculum*. History Education Group: University of East Anglia.

ILEA (1983) Language and history in *History and Social Sciences at Secondary Level, 2*. London: ILEA, reprinted in H. Bourdillon (1994) *Teaching History*, pp. 122–5. London: Routledge, for the Open University.

Jenkins, K. (1991) *Rethinking History*. London: Routledge.

Jenkins, K. (1996) *On 'What is History?': from Carr and Elton to Rorty and White*. London: Routledge.

John, P. (1993) History Tasks at Key Stage 3: a survey from five schools. *Teaching History*, 70: 18–21.

John, P. (1994) Academic tasks in history classrooms. *Research in Education*, 51: 11–22.

Jones, P. (1988) *Lipservice: the story of talk in schools*. Milton Keynes: Open University Press.

Kedourie, H. (1987) *The Errors and Evils of the New History*. London: Centre for Policy Studies.

Kemeny, H. (ed.) (1993) *Learning Together Through Talk: Key Stages 3 and 4*. London: Hodder and Stoughton, for the National Curriculum Project.

Keneally, T. (1983) *Schindler's Ark*. London: Hodder and Stoughton.

Kuper, A. (1988) *The Invention of Primitive Society*. London and New York: Routledge.

Labbett, B.D.C. (1990) Muriel Wakefield. *Cambridge Journal of Education*, 20(3): 207–22.

Labbett, B.D.C. (1979) Towards a curriculum specification for history. *Journal of Curriculum Studies*, 11(2): 125–37.

LaCapra, D. (1983) *Rethinking Intellectual History: texts, contexts, language*. Ithaca: Cornell University Press.

LaCapra, D. (1985) *History and Criticism*. Ithaca: Cornell University Press.

Lee, P.J. (1991) Historical knowledge and the national curriculum in R. Aldrich (ed.) *History in the National Curriculum*. London: Kogan Page, Bedford Way Papers.

Lee, P.J. and Ashby, R. (1987) Children's concepts of empathy and understanding in history in C. Portal (ed.) *The History Curriculum for Teachers*. Falmer: Lewes.

Leff, G. (1969) *History and Social Theory*. London: Merlin Press.

Leitch, V.P. (1983) *Deconstructive Criticism*. New York: Columbia University Press.

Leith, D. (1983) *A Social History of English*. London: Routledge.

Levine, N. (1981) *Language Teaching and Learning: History*. London: Ward Lock.

Lewis, J. (1969 edn) *The Wife of Martin Guerre*. London: Rapp and Carroll.

Little, V. and John, T. (1990) *Historical Fiction in the Classroom*. London: Historical Association, Teaching of History Series, 59.

Lively, P. (1978) Children and the art of memory. *Horn Book Magazine*, 54: 17–23.

Lively, P. (1979) *Treasures of Time*. London: Heinemann.

Lomas, T. (1990) *Teaching and Assessing Historical Understanding*. London: Historical Association.

Low-Beer, A. (1989) Empathy and history. *Teaching History*, 55: 8–12.

Lowenthal, D. (1985) *The Past is a Foreign Country*. Cambridge: Cambridge University Press.

Macfarlane, A. (1978) *The Origins of English Individualism*. Oxford: Blackwell.

Mailer, N. (1968) *The Armies of the Night*. London: Weidenfeld and Nicholson.

Martin, N. *et al.* (1976) *Writing and Learning Across the Curriculum 11–16*. London: Ward Lock.

Marwick, A. (1970) *The Nature of History*. London: Macmillan.

McClure, M., Phillips, T. and Wilkinson, A. (eds) (1988) *Oracy Matters*. Milton Keynes: Open University Press.

McGill, J. (1988) In the history classroom in J. Hickman and K. Kimberley *Teachers, Language and Learning*. London: Routledge.

McManus, P. (1991) Making sense of exhibits in G. Kavanagh (ed.) *Museum Languages: objects and texts*, pp. 35–48, Leicester: Leicester University Press.

Medley, R. and White, C. (1991) Assessing the national curriculum: lessons from assessing history. *Curriculum Journal*, 3(1): 63–74.

Merriman, N. (1991) *Beyond the Glass Case*. Leicester: Leicester University Press.

Moffett, J. (1968) *Teaching the Universe of Discourse*. New York: Houghton Mifflin.

Morris, C. (1992) Opening doors: learning history through talk in T. Booth, W. Swann, M. Masterton and P. Potts (eds) *Learning for All. 1: Curricula for Diversity in Education*. London: Routledge.

New South Wales Department of Education (1987) *Writing K-12*. Sydney, NSW: NSWDE.

Norman, K. (ed.) (1992) *Thinking Voices: the work of the National Oracy Project*. London: Hodder and Stoughton, for the National Curriculum Council.

Norris, C. (1991) *Deconstruction: Theory and Practice* (3rd edn). London and New York: Routledge.

Novick, P. (1988) *That Noble Dream: the objectivity question and the American historical profession*. Cambridge: Cambridge University Press.

Parker, S. (1993) *The Craft of Writing*. London: Paul Chapman.

Pearson, A. and Aloysius, C. (1994) *The Big Foot: museums and children with learning difficulties*. London: British Museum Press.

Perera, K. (1984) *Children's Writing and Reading: analysing classroom language*. Oxford: Blackwell, in association with Deutsch.

Pocock. J.G.A. (1970) Working on ideas in time in L.P. Curtis (ed.) *The Historian's Workshop*. New York: Knopf.

Portal, C. (1987) Empathy as an objective for history teaching in C. Portal (ed.) *The History Curriculum for Teachers*, pp. 89–112. Lewes, Falmer.

Price, M. (1968) History in danger. *History*, 53: 342–7.

Prins, G. (1991) Oral history in P.Burke (ed.) *New Perspectives on Historical Writing*, pp. 110–29. Oxford: Polity Press.

Samuel, R. *et al.* (1990a) History the nation and the schools. *History Workshop Journal*, 29: 92–133.

Samuel, R. *et al.* (1990b) History the nation and the schools. *History Workshop Journal*, 30: 75–128.

Sansom, C. (1987) A developmental approach to the history syllabus in C. Portal (ed.) *The History Curriculum for Teachers*. Lewes: Falmer.

Saxton, J. and Morgan, N. (1994) *Asking Better Questions*. London: Drake Publishing.

SCDC (1989) *The National Writing Project 1: Writing and Learning*. London: Schools Curriculum Development Committee.

Schama, S. (1989) *Citizens: a chronicle of the French Revolution*. New York: Knopf.

Schama, S. (1992) *Dead Certainties: unwarranted speculations*. Cambridge: Granta Publications.

Schools Council (1976) *A New Look at History*. Edinburgh: Holmes McDougall.

Shanks, M. (1991) *Experiencing the Past: on the character of archaeology*. London: Routledge.

Shanks, M. (1996) *Classical Archaeology of Greece: experiences of the discipline*. London: Routledge.

Sheeran, Y. and Barnes, D. (1991) *School writing: discovering the ground rules*. Milton Keynes: Open University Press.

Shemilt, D. (1980) *History 13–16 Evaluation Study*. Edinburgh: Holmes McDougall.

Shemilt, D. (1983) The devil's locomotive. *History and Theory*, 22(1): 1–18.

Shemilt, D. (1984) Beauty and the philosopher: empathy in history and the classroom in A.K. Dickinson, P.J. Lee and P.Rogers, (eds) *Learning History*. London: Heinemann.

Skidelsky, R. (1988a) A question of values. *Times Educational Supplement*, 27 May 1988.

Skidelsky, R. (1988b) History as social engineering. *The Independent*, 1 March 1988.

Slater, J. (1989) 'The Politics of History Teaching: A Humanity Dehumanized?' Special Professorial Lecture, London: Institute of Education.

Slater, J. (1995) *Teaching History in the New Europe*. London: Cassell and Council of Europe.

Southern, R.W. (1977) 'The Historical Experience'. Rede Lecture, 1977. *Times Literary Supplement*, 24 June 1977.

Spencer, E. (1983) *Writing Matters Across the Curriculum*. London: Hodder and Stoughton.

Stone, L. (1979) The revival of narrative. *Past and Present*, 85: 3–24.

Strom, M.S. and Parsons, W.S. (1982) *Facing History and Ourselves: holocaust and human behaviour*. New York: International Education.

Styles, M. (1989) *Collaboration and Writing*. Milton Keynes: Open University Press.

Sutton, C. (1992) *Words, Science and Learning*. Milton Keynes: Open University Press.

Sword, F. (1994) Points of contact. *Journal of Education in Museums*, 15: 7–9.

Sylvester, D. (1994) Change and continuity in history teaching, 1900–

1993 in H. Bourdillon (ed.) *Teaching History*, pp. 9–25. London: Routledge, for the Open University.

Thompson, E.P. (1978) *The Poverty of Theory*. London: Merlin Press.

Thorpe, A. (1992) *Ulverton*. London: Secker and Warburg.

Tosh, J. (1984) *The Pursuit of History: aims, methods and new directions in the study of modern history*. London and New York: Longman.

Trevelyan, G.O. (1876) *Life and Letters of Macaulay*, Volume 2, pp. 37, 249, 281, 385.

Vansina, J. (1974) The power of systematic doubt in historical enquiry. *History in Africa*, 1(1): 109–27.

Vansina, J. (1978) *Oral Tradition as History*. Oxford: Oxford University Press.

Waterhouse, P. (1983) *Managing the Learning Process*. London: McGraw-Hill.

Wells, G. (1992) The centrality of talk in education in K. Norman (ed.) *Thinking Voices: the work of the National Oracy Project*. London: Hodder and Stoughton, for the National Curriculum Council.

West, R. (1988) The making of the English working past: a critical view of the Ironbridge Gorge Museum in R. Lumley (ed.) *The Museum Time Machine*. London: Routledge.

White, H. (1973) *Metahistory*. Baltimore: Johns Hopkins Press.

White, H. (1978) *Tropics of Discourse*. Baltimore: Johns Hopkins Press.

White, H. (1987) *The Content of the Form*. Baltimore: Johns Hopkins Press.

Williams, R. (1983) *Keywords*. Fontana: London.

Wilson, A. (1993) A critical portrait of social history in A. Wilson (ed.) *Rethinking Social History: English society 1570–1920 and its interpretation*, pp. 9–43. Manchester: Manchester University Press.

Wilson, M.D. (1985) *History for Pupils with Learning Difficulties*. London: Hodder and Stoughton.

Wineburg, S. (1991) On the reading of historical texts: notes on the breach between School and Academy. *American Education Research Journal*, 28(3): 499–515.

Wineburg S. and Wilson, S. (1991) Subject matter knowledge in the teaching of history. *Advances in Research in Teaching*, Volume 2, pp. 305–47. Greenwich, Connecticut: JAI Press.

Wood, D. (1992) Teaching talk: how modes of teacher talk affect pupil participation in K. Norman (ed.) op. cit., pp. 203–6.

Wright, P. (1985) *On Living in an Old Country*. London: Verso.

Index

TEACHERS TALK ABOUT TEACHING
COPING WITH CHANGE IN TURBULENT TIMES

Judith Bell (ed.)

This book considers the impact of some of the far-reaching educational reforms introduced in the UK during the last decade, from the point of view of those people who have been required to implement them. All the contributors are, or were, teachers and all are committed to providing the best possible education for school students. Their views on the impact of some of the reforms provide an insight into what it is like to work in schools today and the effect the many demands placed on them have had on their lives. They consider the impact of the National Curriculum (and the associated methods of assessment), career prospects, appraisal, the changed role of governors, the influence of Local Management of Schools and the low morale of many teachers. Throughout the books, the unifying threads are how teachers are coping with change and ways in which their interpretation of autonomy and professionalism differ from those of some ministers and administrators. These messages from the 'coalface' are worthy of serious consideration by all who have a concern for quality education and for the well-being of learners and teachers alike.

Contents
Introduction – PART 1: Changing teaching: Teachers coping with change – Teachers out of control – Teachers autonomy under siege? – PART 2: Careering teachers: New to teaching – In mid-career – From middle to senior management – Leaving the profession – Revisiting classrooms – PART 3: Moving to local management: Not all plain sailing – Governors and teachers: The costs of LMS – PART 4: Subject to change: Careers education: The fight for recognition – At the Core: 'Oh to be in England!' – Postscript – References – Index.

Contributors
Judith Bell, Ken Bryan, Rosemary Chapman, Karen Cowley, Ann Hanson, Jill Horder, Gill Richardson, John Ross, Andrew Spencer, Peter Swientozielskyj, Lorna Unwin, Stephen Waters.

144 pp   0 335 19174 6 (Paperback)

TEACHERS' STORIES

David Thomas (ed.)

In *Teachers' Stories* David Thomas and his contributors present an argument for the content and process of teacher training to be enriched by the inclusion of educational biography, both general (grounded Life Histories) and subject specific accounts, as significant ingredients to be stirred in with more formal theoretic and practical aspects of training. Creating educational biographies is one way of introducing students to critical reflection on their 'taken-for-granted' educational beliefs and values, and their origins.

Though not a training manual, *Teachers' Stories* will be of interest to all teacher trainers including the new cohort of trainees – the teacher mentors. Students will also find support for their attempts to introduce, through journals, diaries or logs, their individual experiences as alternative voices to the pre-eminent discourses of the training institution. It is suggested that such opportunities are especially valuable for students and tutors where the student's background and culture provide unusually distinctive experiences with possibilities for course enrichment as well as personal development.

Contents

Introduction – Treasonable or trustworthy text: Reflections on teacher narrative studies – My language experience – The pupil experience: A view from both sides – An education biography and commentary – What do I do next? – Autobiography, feminism and the practice of action research – Making the private public – Crossing borders for professional development: Narratives of exchange teachers – Breaking tradition: The experiences of an alternative teacher in a rural school – Empirical authors, liminal texts and model readers – Keys to the past – and to the future – 'Composing a life': Women's stories of their careers – Index.

Contributors

Kath Aspinwall, Waltraud Boxall, Arda L. Cole, Florence Gersten, Morwenna Griffiths, Mary Jean Ronan Herzog, J. Gary Knowles, Doreen Littlewood, Anne Murray, Jennifer Nias, David Thomas, Elizabeth Thomas, Peter J. Woods.

240 pp   0 335 19254 8 (Paperback)   0 335 19255 6 (Hardback)